175c

3

STEVENSON, ROBERT LOUIS
"AN OLD SONG" & EDIFYING
LETTERS OF THE RUTHERFORD
FAMILY

($17.50)

WAYNE PUBLIC LIBRARY
MAIN LIBRARY
475 Valley Road
Wayne, N. J.   07470

Books may be returned at any
branch of the library.

AUG 27 1982

AUG 27 1982

AN OLD SONG

and

EDIFYING LETTERS OF THE RUTHERFORD FAMILY

a newly discovered long story

AN OLD SONG

and a previously unpublished short story

EDIFYING LETTERS OF THE RUTHERFORD FAMILY

by Robert Louis Stevenson

Edited and with an Introduction
by Roger G. Swearingen

ARCHON BOOKS   WILFION BOOKS, PUBLISHERS
HAMDEN, CONNECTICUT   PAISLEY, SCOTLAND
1982

© 1982 Roger G. Swearingen   All rights reserved

First published 1982 in the USA by Archon Books
an imprint of The Shoe String Press, Inc.
995 Sherman Avenue
Hamden, Connecticut
and in Scotland by Wilfion Books
12 Townhead Terrace
Paisley, Renfrewshire PA1 2AX

LIBRARY OF CONGRESS CATALOGING IN PUBLICATION DATA

Stevenson, Robert Louis, 1850-1894
   A newly discovered long story, An old song, and a previously unpublished
short story, Edifying letters of the Rutherford family.

      Includes bibliographical references.
      I. Swearingen, Roger G., 1944-   . II. Stevenson,
   Robert Louis, 1850-1894. An old song. 1982.
   III. Stevenson, Robert Louis, 1850-1894. Edifying
   letters of the Rutherford family. 1982. IV. Title.
   PR5481.S94   823'.8   82-1627
   Archon ISBN 0-208-01973-1   AACR2
   Wilfion ISBN 0-905075-12-9

Printed in the United States of America

Cover design by Craig Maclachlan

CONTENTS

INTRODUCTION

Few scholarly discoveries are as exciting as finding an important, entirely unknown work by an author whom one has been studying for years. Thanks to the unrivaled completeness of the Robert Louis Stevenson collections at Yale University, both in Sterling Memorial Library and in the Edwin J. Beinecke Robert Louis Stevenson Collection in the Beinecke Rare Book and Manuscript Library, this pleasure was recently mine. A serial story of a dozen chapters published anonymously in the weekly *London* in 1877, *An Old Song*, can now be identified not only as written by Stevenson but in fact as his first published story, antedating *A Lodging for the Night (Temple Bar*, October 1877) by some six months. Moreover, based as it appears to be on *The Two Falconers of Cairnstane*, a story which Stevenson mentions in a letter of November 1874, *An Old Song* is arguably also the earliest work of fiction by Stevenson to have survived except for a few stories he wrote during his childhood.[1] Its publication in the present volume thus represents its first appearance ever under Stevenson's own name, and its first appearance anywhere since it was first published—anonymously—in 1877. The attribution of *An Old Song* is certain, thanks to the preservation in the Beinecke Collection of a single folio leaf of Stevenson's manuscript (Beinecke 6106). Numbered 23 at the top, this single, untitled leaf contains the end of Chapter 6 and the beginning of Chapter 7 of a story which proves to be *An Old Song*.

throwing the great coat over him, fled back into the house. There
never was a night like that, at Grangehead, Mr John slept
on the gravel plot, Mr Malcolm slept by the dining room fire,
and the Colonel sat up all night in his own room in
meditation and religious exercise. There was no tea, and
no family worship.

Chapter VII.

The Colonel hung his head from that day forward. He turned
suddenly and surprisingly bald; there were broken tones in
his voice; his face seemed to have shrunk; and he
sometimes smiled wanderingly. Malcolm never uttered John's
name in his uncle's presence; but he thought
of him often enough, as he looked upon these changes. The
old man had been stabbed to the heart; the ...
... slower or faster, he was
dying.

There can be no doubt that he kept up an acquaintance
with John's life, and secretly helped him. But if he was pleased
at rendering assistance, he must have been deeply pained
by all he heard; any bulletin must have been another cowardly
blow on his white hairs; for John's be new life was one of which
the Colonel could not but condemn.

The end came, when the two lads were in their twenty first
year; John writing leaders-notes in a London newspaper; and
Malcolm agreeably & conscious of his approaching marriage with
Mary Rolland. The Colonel took to his bed rather suddenly. It was
wild windy weather, and the sky was full of flying vapours.
He had been looking out of the window ... all
afternoon; and towards dusk he called to Malcolm and pointed
to the labouring trees and the dead leaves whistling in the
open.

"I'm too old and tired for this sort of thing," he said.
"I think I'll go to bed." He looked at Malcolm queerly. "I
don't mean to get up again," he added. And he kept his

Facsimile of the only surviving manuscript page of *An Old Song*. Beinecke Rare Book and Manuscript Library, Yale University.

My discovery of this story more than a century after it was written and published vindicates the maxim with which Stevenson himself closed *An Inland Voyage* (1878) a year later: "the most beautiful adventures are not those we go to seek." I was not looking for *An Old Song*, or indeed for anything in particular. My reason for reading *London* at all was the same reason Yale surely had in acquiring for Sterling Library a photostatic copy of the entire run of the magazine some years ago from the British Museum: Stevenson had been associated with *London* from the beginning of its short life. In 1878, a year after it began publication—the first issue appeared on 3 February 1877, the last of 114 weekly issues on 5 April 1879—Stevenson had published anonymously in *London* three essays later collected in *Virginibus Puerisque* (1881): *A Plea for Gas Lamps* (27 April 1878), *Pan's Pipes* (4 May), and *El Dorado* (11 May). Later in the same year, he published under his own name the stories later collected as the first volume of *New Arabian Nights* (2 volumes, 1882) and the story reprinted as *Providence and the Guitar* in the second volume of that collection. During the mid-1960s, Ernest J. Mehew identified as Stevenson's six more anonymous contributions to *London*, four essays and two reviews published in the first four issues of the magazine in 1877.[2] So far as then was known, these essays, stories, and reviews—some anonymous, others signed, some reprinted, others not—comprised the whole of Stevenson's contributions to *London*. No doubt Stevenson had contributed, as his wife recalled, some extempore verse to help fill empty columns,[3] and perhaps too he had written a few short prose pieces now and then.[4] But it seemed unlikely that any important contributions of his to *London* had gone unnoticed.

Founded toward the end of 1876, *London* was chiefly the inspiration of Robert Glasgow Brown. Stevenson and Brown had been at the University of Edinburgh together in the early 1870s, but a stronger connection was through William Ernest Henley. Henley was virtually the cofounder of *London*, he took over the editorship from Brown very soon after publication began, and he presided over the magazine's eventual demise two years later in 1879. Stevenson and Henley had been friends for almost two years when *London* was founded, ever since Leslie Stephen had brought Stevenson to Henley's bedside in the Royal Infirmary, Edinburgh, on 12 February 1875.5 No doubt it was chiefly through Henley that Stevenson became associated with *London* during the earliest stages of its life.

The magazine was aggressively Conservative. A quotation from Disraeli about the city of London appeared on the masthead: "A great city, whose image dwells in the memory of man." In the first issue the magazine's editorial policy was declared in part as follows:

> To have no creed at all is fatal to the influence of a journal; to have a timid creed is trying to its honesty. But in the opinion represented by [this] . . . new journal the forces and feelings of the nation are ultimately Conservative.

And this declaration was followed by a long article praising in the most lavish terms the "brilliant and complex personality . . . of Lord Beaconsfield" *(London, 3 February 1877, p. 3)*. The leading articles each week were political. Pugnaciously Tory in spirit, the anonymous writers (chiefly Henley and Brown, at the outset) took obvious and enormous pleasure in savaging the latest words and deeds of Liberal politicians in and out of Parliament. After the political articles came a section on finance, as often as not in the form of a continuing series evaluating some kind of personal investment such as life insurance. These articles too were anonymous, as were those on the arts which made up the balance of every issue: theater, fine arts, music, and book reviews, essays on various general topics, poetry, and usually an essay in a continuing series such as that on contemporary women authors.

Introduction

One additional feature of the arts contributions in *London* was the weekly "Feuilleton," an installment of a longer work of fiction run serially. *An Old Song*, the second such work, commenced publication in the fourth issue of *London* and ran for four weeks; and like those before and after it during the first eight months of *London* it was published anonymously. The first signed "Feuilleton" in *London* was Emile Gaboriau's *The Orcival Murder*, in English translation, and it ran from 22 September 1877 through 1 June 1878. It was followed by Stevenson's *Latter-Day Arabian Nights* (8 June–26 October) and *Léon Berthilini's Guitar* (2–23 November), both signed, Stevenson's only signed contributions to *London*.

As I have remarked already, I was reading *London* strictly to get an idea of the kind of magazine it was. Although Stevenson had been writing fiction for nearly a decade before 1877, there was no reason to think that he had contributed anything to *London* except the various pieces already identified. As for the crucial manuscript leaf, I had examined and transcribed it years before in writing my doctoral dissertation on Stevenson (Yale, 1970), and more recently I had again consigned it to the not unpopulated limbo of stories and other manuscript fragments which Stevenson had worked on at one time or another and then abandoned— this in preparing my complete study of the composition and publication of all of Stevenson's prose works, *The Prose Writings of Robert Louis Stevenson: A Guide* (Archon/Macmillan, 1980). Needless to say, this error has now been corrected, and *An Old Song* is now duly listed under its own name.

My discovery of *An Old Song*, in short, was a happy accident. Reading through *London* issue by issue from the beginning, naturally I came upon *An Old Song*. At first glance, it seemed unremarkable enough, and it was not actually until I came to the second installment that it struck me that violent emotions and characters named John, Malcolm, and the Colonel also figured in a manuscript fragment I had seen many years before. The second installment ended with the fifth chapter. Heroically, I resisted the temptation to skip ahead—dutifully, if perhaps a trifle more rapidly than before, paging through the political and other material which preceded the crucial next installment of *An Old Song*. Sure enough, when I came to the sixth and seventh chapters, the published material corresponded exactly with what I remembered of the manuscript fragment, a fact which it was a pleasure to confirm in detail from the manuscript itself next morning in the Beinecke Library.[6]

Further confirmation that the story was Stevenson's came a few weeks later, when Ernest J. Mehew brought to my attention an undated, unpublished letter from Stevenson to Robert Glasgow Brown in the National Library of Scotland, a letter which Mr. Mehew has now been able to assign confidently to early or mid-February 1877. Brown was evidently not pleased with Stevenson's work in *London*, and in reply Stevenson remarked:

> I shall give you the Feuilleton as fast as I can with personal convenience. As for reading three volumes and writing an article in two days, I shall make an attempt this once without promising success; but I must ask you not to put me again in the same position.
>
> As neither of us are very much pleased with my productions, I should think the best way would be to cease them *quam primum*. Mind you, I don't desert; I only say as soon as you are able to fill the place I have unworthily occupied, the better for your paper and my own comfort.[7]

The discovery of *An Old Song* also clarified a remark of Stevenson's which had long puzzled Mr. Mehew and me. To George Iles, Stevenson had written on 29 October 1887: "My first story (that I dared to reprint) was 'Will o' the Mill,' written in France."[8]

No published but unreprinted early story by Stevenson was known, but Stevenson's reference was clear. Now it can be seen that he had in mind *An Old Song*—if not perhaps still another undiscovered story or stories.

As a literary work, *An Old Song* is a curious production; and especially in the light of Stevenson's letter to Brown it seems likely that it was in fact a story which Stevenson had written some time before, then hastily retouched and pressed into the service of a fledgling magazine not oversupplied with contributions or contributors. The main characters are John and Malcolm Falconer of Grangehead and their guardian Colonel Falconer, and these surnames suggest that it was to this story Stevenson was referring when in November 1874 he included *The Two Falconers of Cairnstane* in a list of twelve stories by him, already written or drafted, which might be published together as *A Book of Stories*. *The Two Falconers of Cairnstane* was one of four Scottish stories projected for the collection, and it was, Stevenson said in November 1874, complete except for "a few pages."⁹ He soon gave up the idea of publishing *A Book of Stories*. As he remarked three months later, in February 1875:

> I am *pioching*, like a madman, at my stories, and can make
> nothing of them; my simplicity is tame and dull—my
> passion tinsel, boyish, hysterical. Never mind—ten
> years hence, if I live, I shall have learned, so help me
> God.¹⁰

Probably this story, like the others, was simply laid aside for the next two years, until Stevenson hastily rewrote it, as *An Old Song*, to fill space in the early issues of *London* in 1877.¹¹

Set in Scotland in the present or recent past (the only year dates are given simply as "18—"), *An Old Song* is a grim, and at times merely bitter, story of mutual misapprehensions and distorted motives which years later, when the truth is revealed,

cause mere unconstructive pain. None of the characters comes off
with much credit, each having contributed to (without being the
sole cause of) the misery of himself and others through weakness,
misunderstanding, self-delusion, or some unfathomable perversity of character. Nor does the story seem to have any other aim
than to set these characters, their limitations and their unhappi-
ness, before us: such things do occur, and there is little one can
do to prevent or avoid them. Not even religious fanaticism can
be blamed. John's original misunderstanding, Stevenson points
out, is chiefly due to his youthful inexperience, and to Malcolm's
and Mary's. For as Stevenson remarked years later:

> Life is not all Beer and Skittles; and mine is closing in
> dark enough. What is left, my God, in such a welter?
> When does blame come in? Nowhere, I believe, or very
> little. Only the inherent tragedy of things works itself
> out from white to black and blacker, and the poor things
> of a day look ruefully on.[12]

There is no particular reason why these things happen. They
simply do.

Stevenson relies heavily on melodramatic contrivance in *An
Old Song*: the Colonel's deathbed injunction, the reappearance of
the key, the coming to light of Mary's poem at just the wrong
moment. The various scenes and conversations could be trans-
ferred to the stage almost without change. And the characters are
but shallowly explored. Their attributes, whether of melancholy,
youth, superficiality, or fanaticism, are given to them chiefly
because they are needed in the plot. Stevenson shows us hardly
anything of how these attributes affect his characters' lives apart
from their immediate dealings with one another. John's journalis-
tic career finds him vacating posts just as the papers themselves
are about to collapse, and possibly his behaviour at Grangehead
is to be seen as parallel. The Colonel's youthful wildness is per-

haps to be seen as replicated in John's. But with these exceptions Stevenson uses characterization only to supply in the actors the few attributes they must have if the plot is to unfold as he wishes. Most of the same limitations, it might be added, are apparent in *When the Devil Was Well*, Stevenson's only other surviving story of this early date. Both justify his own harsh remark, already quoted, that "my simplicity is tame and dull—my passion tinsel, boyish, hysterical."

The significance of *An Old Song* lies elsewhere. Its artistic limitations, as they were to Stevenson, are obvious. Above all, *An Old Song* gives the lie to the supposition that Stevenson's dim view of human nature and human possibility came late—not until *Dr. Jekyll and Mr. Hyde* (written in 1885), for instance, or *The Master of Ballantrae* (1887-89), or even *The Ebb–Tide* (1893) or *Weir of Hermiston* (1892-94). Clearly he is no more hopeful about the possibilities of human happiness in *An Old Song*, written when he was in his mid–twenties, than ten or even fifteen years later. *An Old Song* is perhaps unconvincingly, melodramatically grim compared to these later works. But the view is nevertheless the same. Grimness was a mode of imagining to which Stevenson had access from the beginning.

Second, *An Old Song* shows that even in his twenties Stevenson had the same view of fiction that by the end of the century, in part due to his own arguments for it from *Victor Hugo's Romances* (1874) onward, was all but universally accepted: that the writer's job was to render, not explain, to depict rather than also draw practical and moral conclusions. *An Old Song* is remarkable for its ending, and for what might be called its pointlessness. The story has no moral, except perhaps to be other than what we cannot help being, and in the final scene John gets revenge, and Malcolm humiliating punishment, without any intimation that in either case justice has at last been done. As the story's proverbial title suggests, this is an old story, familiar without being profound. Of Malcolm's state at the end of the story we might well remark as Stevenson had of Gilliat's struggle in the toils of the octopus in Victor Hugo's *Les Travailleurs de la mer* six months before he first took up this story in 1874: "here, indeed, is the true position of man in the universe."[13]

Finally, *An Old Song* is notable for the appearance in it, as nowhere else in Stevenson's early fiction, of two linked motifs which clearly had a powerful hold on his literary imagination: the motif of brothers (in this instance, cousins), and the motif of nemesis, the one brother returning ultimately to destroy the other. In one later version, these motifs obviously appear in *Dr. Jekyll and Mr. Hyde*; in another, explicitly, in *The Master of Ballantrae*. Versions of the brothers motif may also be seen in such pairings as David and Alan in *Kidnapped* (1886) and in the enforced intimacy of such "crews" as one finds in *Treasure Island* (1881) or *The Ebb–Tide*. Neither motif is unfamiliar to students of popular melodrama or of Romanticism in the eighteenth and nineteenth centuries; and indeed one might well argue that one of Stevenson's most distinctive habits as a writer is his fondness for resurrecting and reusing old motifs and forms. Both of these motifs, moreover, afford ample excuse for confrontations, a kind of scene at which Stevenson excelled, and of which he was particularly fond. Where there is intimacy, there will be confrontation, all the more so when one character has both a desire and the willingness, even after many years, to cause the other harm.

Thus one can only speculate whether there is not also an intimate personal dimension to *An Old Song*, a dimension of personal preoccupation if not indeed displaced autobiography. Only in his unbending adherence to principle does the Colonel resemble Stevenson's father; but even so we may find in his concealed understanding of John's motives, despite his unwillingness to act on it, a hopeful wish or guess of Stevenson's own about his father's continuing distress over his religious opinions and restless-

ly unconventional behavior. Where there was estrangement, perhaps nevertheless there was also understanding and love. The
linked motifs of brothers and nemesis, we may speculate, origi-
nate in self-doubt and guilt: in the feeling, to which Stevenson's
letters of this period and afterwards bear witness, that perhaps
after all his father was right. His belief in himself, and in his own
integrity, was mere self-satisfaction. Like Malcolm's it was based
on an illusion which must inevitably shatter. And his own worst
enemy was himself. That the agent of Malcolm's disillusionment
should be his cousin/brother, we may speculate, originates in
Stevenson's own feeling that the selfish, reckless, anarchic part of
his nature would at length be the honorable part's undoing. Later,
in *Dr. Jekyll and Mr. Hyde* and *The Master of Ballantrae*, Stevenson
would find the technical means to universalize these preoccupa-
tions, to make us perceive that they are also our own. *An Old Song*
is thus only a first attempt; for many reasons it fails to move us
deeply; but thematically it anticipates much in Stevenson's later
work.

The second work in the present volume, *Edifying Letters of the
Rutherford Family*, is published here for the first time, from the
unfinished manuscript in the Edwin J. Beinecke Robert Louis
Stevenson Collection at Yale University (Beinecke 6185). Out-
lined and begun at about the same time as *An Old Song* was revised
for publication, the *Edifying Letters* are directly, indeed transpar-
ently, autobiographical. Nowhere outside of his letters of the
period to his cousin Bob Stevenson, to Charles Baxter, and later
to Mrs. Sitwell, does Stevenson write as fully about his own
deeply trying experiences during his early twenties in Edinburgh. If in *An Old Song* autobiography is transmuted and displaced, in the *Edifying Letters* it is often all too near the surface.

Stevenson's one–page notebook outline of the *Edifying Letters*
(Beinecke 6184, notebook 52) lists seven characters and eleven

letters to be exchanged between them. The manuscript itself, eight folio leaves written on both sides of the page in ink, contains three of these letters and part of a fourth, and the correspondence involves five of the characters listed in the outline. William Rutherford, the son, is obviously Stevenson himself. Paul Somerset, traveling abroad, is Stevenson's cousin Bob—Robert Alan Mowbray Stevenson—upon whom Stevenson later modeled another Paul Somerset, in *The Dynamiter* (1885). James Rutherford, the father, is Stevenson's father Thomas Stevenson, and Professor Daubeny Fisher is probably his close friend Professor William Swan of the University of St. Andrews. Young Rutherford's intimate friend in Edinburgh, Charles Butler, is plainly Stevenson's classmate at the University of Edinburgh, Charles Baxter, his lifelong friend and legal adviser.

Such harrowing interviews between son and parents as the one narrated in William Rutherford's first letter occurred often between Stevenson and his own parents during the early 1870s—never more strenuously, perhaps, than in 1873, a year which ended with Stevenson's being sent by Dr. Andrew Clark to winter alone at Mentone on the French Riviera. In her recent *RLS: A Life Study* (1980), Jenni Calder quotes two paragraphs from the *Edifying Letters* as elucidating Stevenson's long letter to Charles Baxter on 2 February 1873 describing one extremely painful recent interview between Stevenson and his father on the subject of religion.[14] On 7 October 1873, two weeks before he went down to London to see Dr. Clark, Stevenson summarized his whole situation in a letter to Miss E. R. Crosby:

> ... my life is a very distressing one at home, so distressing that I have a great difficulty in keeping up a good heart at all or even in keeping my health together. For nearly a year back, I have lived in the most miserable contention with my parents on the subject of religion.

Facsimile of the first page of *Edifying Letters of the Rutherford Family*. Beinecke Rare Book and Manuscript Library, Yale University.

I can do nothing myself, but hold my peace and try to
steer away from dangerous subjects; but even with all
this, the fires break out every now and again and I am
driven to the most wretched state. To be continually
told that you have utterly wrecked the lives of your
father and mother, and to see that much of this is true—
the wretched truth—, is not you must grant, a very
favourable circumstance for cheerful thought.[15]

Religion is not the point of contention in the interview which
William Rutherford describes in his first letter—rather it is "our
old chronic irritation of late hours"—but the next two letters
nonetheless make it clear both how deeply religious the elder
Rutherford, like Thomas Stevenson, was, and how torn between
affection and unease the son kept finding himself. "I tell you
frankly, Charles," William Rutherford writes in the third letter,
". . . if he had not touched me so nearly with his gentleness with
Nath, I might have risked a walk with him; but as things are, I
could trust neither him nor myself; we should have been safe to
grow confidential; and confidence, where there is so great a gulf
in sympathy, means quarrelling." Such, clearly, were Stevenson's own relations with his father during the early 1870s.

One can only guess at the plot which Stevenson had in mind
for the *Edifying Letters of the Rutherford Family.* As a literary work,
it scarcely gets underway before it breaks off. But if Stevenson's
own experiences are a reliable guide, the elder Rutherford's com-
placent belief that he is his son's *"friend* rather than his *father"* will
shortly be shattered by disclosures from the dying young cousin
Nathaniel. In particular these disclosures will probably concern
the society, called the L. J. R., about which William Rutherford
writes at length in the third of the *Edifying Letters,* and Paul
Somerset's undesirable influence upon William. For precisely
such disclosures were made—if not about the L. J. R., certainly

about Bob Stevenson's supposedly malign influence on Stevenson—in a posthumous letter to Stevenson's father, written by a dying cousin of Stevenson's in late August or early September 1873.

"Bob . . . was a 'blight' and a 'mildew,' " Stevenson wrote to Mrs. Sitwell on 9 September 1873, describing his cousin's remarks, and that evening Thomas Stevenson had to his face accused Bob of "having ruined his house and his son." Stevenson continues:

> Bob answered that he didn't know where I had found out that the Christian religion was not true, but that he hadn't told me. And I think from that point the conversation went off into emotion and never touched shore again. There was not much said about me—my views according to my father are a childish imitation of Bob's, to cease the moment the *mildew* is removed.[16]

No doubt it was toward some such revelation of son to father that Stevenson planned to bring the story of cousin Nathaniel as the *Edifying Letters of the Rutherford Family* eventually unfolded.

From the third of the *Edifying Letters* Stevenson deleted in his draft much of the material about the society, the L. J. R., which young Rutherford and Charles Butler were founding. In the text presented here, these deleted passages are retained, in square brackets, because it is in this third letter that we have undoubtedly the fullest account of the real society, also called the L. J. R. and no doubt identical with the one described here, which Stevenson, Baxter, Sir Walter Simpson, James Walter Ferrier, Bob Stevenson and others actually did found during the early 1870s when most of them were students at the University of Edinburgh. As the *Edifying Letters* makes clear, the initials stood for liberty, justice, and reverence. Among the society's tenets were, it is said, abolition of the House of Lords and the precept, "Disregard everything our parents have ever taught us."[17] Itself preceded by the "Respectable Order of Habbakuk," the L. J. R. was certainly in existence before the spring of 1872; a year later Stevenson wrote an "Inscription for the Tankard of a Society now dissolved"; and though as Charles Baxter recalled probably no more than a dozen meetings were held, the L. J. R. and its principles clearly engaged Stevenson's passionate attention throughout the year or two during the early 1870s when it actually existed.[18] Almost twenty years later Charles Baxter recalled "the fatal ritual" for the L. J. R. which he had invented and the *awful* scene that followed on its discovery" by Stevenson's father: "I still remember meeting you [Stevenson] in the Lothian Road and hearing the terrible news that fell from your blanched lips. I also remember a sensation as if my knees were melting. That was the way terror affected *me.* "[19] No doubt some such discovery of the L. J. R. and its principles was also planned for the later unfolding of the *Edifying Letters of the Rutherford Family*, by way of cousin Nathaniel or by some other means. For it would have contrasted father and son once more, showing again how little the one knew of how the other really felt—a point now made only very crudely in the differences between their two accounts of visiting the dying cousin.

If there is a theme or point made in the *Edifying Letters of the Rutherford Family* as a whole, it is a merely descriptive one. Imaginative, aspiring young men in Scotland find themselves hemmed in on every side. Only in stolen nights "of intellect and sherry," only in founding and arguing about societies such as the L. J. R., only in such "strange waking vision[s]" as William Rutherford describes in the fourth letter—only in ways like these, it would seem, can such young men feel free. Only in such ways—the ways of escape, private rebellion, and reverie—can they feel themselves at home and happy in this world. The rest is nothing but "rain and carping and sour looks, and the damned wearisome ten commandments, and their ten million corollaries, dinned in people's ears to perpetuity." No more than *An Old Song* is the *Edifying Letters of the Rutherford Family* an indictment of Scotland. Even William Rutherford concedes that perhaps there is no such place as the happier, friendlier world of which he dreams; he even prides himself upon having feelings typical of young men everywhere. But both works do explore—however clumsily—reticences, conflicts, misunderstandings, bigotries, beliefs, and tensions among Scottish characters in distinctively Scottish situations. This, I think, is the source of the strange power which both works have to interest or even fascinate us today, despite their many and obvious limitations as works of literature. Both explore that complex Scottish world of which Stevenson is an altogether characteristic product: a world of tension and of love, of escapist longing and remarkable strength.

Thanks are due to Alan Osbourne and to the Beinecke Rare Book and Manuscript Library, Yale University, for permission to publish both of these works from materials in the Yale collections; to Donald Gallup, editor, and the *Yale University Library Gazette*, for permission to use again in this introduction part of my account of finding *An Old Song*, originally published there; and to Ernest J. Mehew for invaluable information on *An Old Song* and important corrections in the final text of the *Edifying Letters of the Rutherford Family*.

NOTES

1. *When the Devil Was Well* (MS., Beinecke 7143) dates from early 1875, whereas *An Old Song*, under its earlier title, dates from November 1874 or a little before. It is a pleasure to record here my thanks to the American Council of Learned Societies for a

grant–in–aid which made possible the research of which this discovery was one result, and to Ernest J. Mehew for supplying valuable supporting information from Stevenson's letters.

2. *Our City Men. No. I.—A Salt-Water Financier* and *The Book of the Week. Mr. Tennyson's 'Harold'*, London, 3 February 1877, pp. 9–10, 18–19; *In the Latin Quarter. No. I.—A Ball at Mr. Elsinare's*, 10 February, pp. 41–42; *In the Latin Quarter. No. II.—A Studio of Ladies*, 17 February, p. 64; *The Paris Bourse* and *The Book of the Week. Wallace's Russia*, 24 February, pp. 88, 92–93. Mehew reprints the third and fifth of these articles in "Two Uncollected Stevenson Contributions to the Magazine *London,*" *The Stevensonian: The Journal of the Robert Louis Stevenson Club*, London, No. 2 (August 1965), pp. 2–7.

3. Fanny Stevenson, "Prefatory Note" to *New Arabian Nights*, in the Tusitala Edition of Stevenson's *Works* (London, 1924), *I*, xxviii–xxix.

4. George L. McKay lists ten possible minor contributions by Stevenson to *London* in his catalogue of the Beinecke Collection, *A Stevenson Library . . .* (1951–64), *6*, 2347–50. None seems to me especially likely to have been written by Stevenson, and the review of Henry Irving's performance in *Richard III, At the Lyceum on Monday*, 3 February 1877, was written by William Ernest Henley.

5. Stevenson's friendship with Henley is reviewed at length in Edward H. Cohen, *The Henley–Stevenson Quarrel* (1974).

6. Beinecke 6106. Written in ink with corrections in ink and pencil, the manuscript is on paper watermarked "A. Pirie & Sons/1874" and comprises 33 lines of prose in Stevenson's hand. It begins with material in the next–to–last paragraph of Chapter 6, "throwing the great coat over him . . . ," continues with the chapter number and beginning of Chapter 7, "The Colonel hung his head from that day forward," and ends part way into the fourth paragraph of Chapter 7, "And he kept his word." Revisions

in the manuscript, for example the transposition of the last two sentences of Chapter 6, are incorporated into the published text.

7.   Stevenson to Brown, National Library of Scotland, Edinburgh. See also Stevenson to Charles Baxter, dated by Mehew as March or April 1877: *"London* is rapidly hustling me into the abhorrèd tomb; I do write such damned rubbish in it, that's a fac', and I hate doing it so inconceivably" (Beinecke 2669, in *RLS: Stevenson's Letters to Charles Baxter*, ed. D. Ferguson and M. Waingrow, 1956, p. 51). To Sidney Colvin he wrote in mid–May 1877: "I've been done with *London,* many's the long day, so you can sleep in peace" (Beinecke 3022). Stevenson thus seems to have severed all connection with *London* after working for it three or four months in 1877, returning only in April 1878 when W.E. Henley was in sole charge of the magazine. Stevenson comments on his friend Professor Fleeming Jenkin's strong objections to his early work in *London* in his *Memoir of Fleeming Jenkin* (1887), Chapter 6.

8.   Published originally, Toronto *Globe,* 27 December 1887; reprinted *The Bookman,* 7 (London, February 1895), 136.

9.   Stevenson to Colvin, November 1874, Beinecke 3006; in Stevenson's *Letters,* Tusitala Edition (London, 1924), 1, 213–14, where it is misdated January 1875. This story is one of three which Stevenson marked with an asterisk, commenting: "The asterisked cusses, I think *capital."*

10.   *Letters, 1,* 216.

11.   *An Old Song* was published in four installments in *London:* 24 February 1877, pp. 82–83 (Chapters 1–3); 3 March, pp. 106–8 (Chapters 4–6); 10 March, pp. 131–32 (Chapters 7–8); 17 March, pp. 152–54 (Chapters 9–12).

12.   Stevenson to Colvin, 23 August 1893, Widener Collection, Houghton Library, Harvard University; partially in *Letters, 5,* 78.

13.   *Victor Hugo's Romances (Cornhill Magazine*, August 1874); in Stevenson's *Works*, Tusitala Edition (London, 1924), *27*, 15.

14.   Stevenson to Baxter, 2 February 1873, Beinecke 2651, in *RLS: Stevenson's Letters to Charles Baxter* (1956), pp. 23-25; Jenni Calder, *RLS: A Life Study* (1980), pp. 59-62. As Calder notes, 1873 was for Stevenson "a climactic year."

15.   Stevenson to Miss E. R. Crosby, 7 October 1873, Beinecke Collection, uncatalogued.

16.   Stevenson to Mrs. Sitwell, 9–10 September 1873, National Library of Scotland; quoted in Roger Lancelyn Green, "Stevenson in Search of a Madonna," *Essays and Studies*, 1950, pp. 130–31.

17.   Graham Balfour, *The Life of Robert Louis Stevenson* (London, 1901), *1*, 90; Mrs. Douglas Maclagan, "Recollections," in *I Can Remember Robert Louis Stevenson*, ed. Rosaline Masson (1922), p. 46. Maclagan only says, however, that the precept about disregarding parents was discovered by Stevenson's father in the "rules for a club of the boy's [RLS's] own forming," not that this club was the L. J. R.

18.   Baxter to Stevenson, 14 July 1886, National Library of Scotland typescript 9891, f. 18; Beinecke 6455–56, two versions of the inscription, the former dated Edin Spring 73. See also *RLS: Stevenson's Letters to Charles Baxter* (1956), pp. 11, 15–16, 33.

19.   Baxter to Stevenson, 23 September 1891, Beinecke 4035, in *RLS: Stevenson's Letters to Charles Baxter* (1956), p. 289 n.1. J. C. Furnas, *Voyage to Windward: The Life of Robert Louis Stevenson* (1951), p. 65, suggests that Thomas Stevenson "had found a copy of the impudent constitution of the L. J. R." and that this was the subject of the discussion with his father which Stevenson described in his letter to Baxter on 2 February 1873. But Baxter's 1891 letter and Stevenson's reply to it both make it clear that the discovery was of Baxter's "ritual" and that the confrontation of father and son on the matter occurred during the day, not at

night. In addition, Stevenson's letter of 2 February 1873, which Furnas quotes in part, actually says nothing about the L. J. R. or its constitution, merely that "in the course of conversation" Stevenson's father "put me one or two questions as to beliefs, which I candidly answered" (Beinecke 2651, in *RLS: Stevenson's Letters to Charles Baxter*, 1956, p. 23; cf. Furnas, p. 65 and see note 17, above).

A NOTE ON THE TEXT

The text of *An Old Song* appears here exactly as it does in the weekly *London,* 24 February–17 March 1877, except that the two references made in Chapter XI to events which occurred on John's "seventeenth" birthday have both been changed to "eighteenth." This brings these references into conformity with Chapter III, where the events are first described. Four obvious printing defects and one typographical error have been corrected: quotation marks missing at the end of the fourteenth paragraph of Chapter I; a full stop missing at the end of the fourth paragraph in Chapter II; the second word, "I," in the third paragraph of Chapter III, and the letter "s" in the word 'described' in the fourth paragraph of Chapter VIII, both missing as printed but with spaces clearly left for them; and a comma mistakenly printed instead of a full stop at the end of the tenth-from-last paragraph of Chapter X. Single quotation marks enclosing words of spoken dialogue have been substituted for the double marks printed originally. The original division by installments was as follows: issue of 24 February 1877, Chapters I–III; 3 March, Chapters IV–V; 10 March, Chapters VI–VIII; 17 March, Chapters IX–XII. Each installment is headed "FEUILLETON," followed by the story's title and the text of that installment.

The text of the *Edifying Letters of the Rutherford Family* appears as it does in Stevenson's manuscript, Beinecke 6185, ignoring deleted material except for the passages on the L. J. R. given here in square brackets (pp. 95–97), and substituting single quotation marks for the double marks which Stevenson used.

An Old Song

CHAPTER I

Lieutenant-Colonel John Falconer broke the traditions of his family by entering the army, and his whole youth was expensive and disastrous. He was near being asked to leave his regiment; he was in trouble about the mess funds; he was deplorably in debt; when his aunt sent him a religious tract, it was returned with a pen and ink commentary in a blunt, military style. By these flashes and reverberations his stormy existence was from time to time revealed to his family at home; and as he never wrote between whiles, a letter from India denoted a new scrape.

Suddenly, at the age of thirty, he was converted at a revival meeting. From that moment he was a changed man. It was his principal boast that he had not once omitted or shortened his devotions since that day, and for those who knew his previous habits, the pretension was imposing in the extreme. At the same time that he became religious he developed a sense of duty, and turned into a good officer. Falconer was counted a trusty man; Napier swore by him; his men feared and admired him in equal parts.

When his father died, and he found himself the last of the family besides two nephews, he took it to be his duty to go home and supervise his nephews and the estate. An unpleasant duty was to him what stolen pleasures are to others: it was his passion; he flung himself into it headlong; and the more unpleasant it was, the higher his pride rose as he performed it. To live at Grangehead, to take care of an estate, to be pestered with a pair of playful urchins, to give up his regiment—this was the best thing of the sort he had yet encountered, the raciest piece of self-sacrifice conceivable, the very pink of martyrdom; and on his homeward voyage Colonel Falconer was a prey to all the delights of what we may call Black Happiness.

His old Aunt Rebecca (who had sent him the tract in former days) still survived in a cottage at Hampstead; she had received in the meantime the two nephews; and so the Colonel's first visit was to her.

Aunt Rebecca was much moved when she saw the new arrival descend with a grave demeanour from a hansom cab. He was very tall, upright, and muscular, with a dash of the trooper—a sort of flavour of sword exercise about his carriage. His face was the colour of genuine Indian curry; his moustache heavy, and quite white; his eyebrows black, bushy, and singularly immobile. About his mouth there lurked a hard expression that was imposing, but a little doubtful; it smacked of the soldier. The Colonel was not a hypocrite, mind you.

Aunt Rebecca was all in a flutter, but he kissed her on the left eyebrow, asked after her in a harrowing voice, and generally put her at her ease again. He sat down, and they began talking of family bereavements.

'My father was not irreligious, of course,' said the Colonel, 'but he scarcely seemed a man of vital piety.'

'He died with great joy,' said Miss Rebecca, answering the question which the other had been afraid to put.

'Thank God,' said the Colonel, with stentorian fervour. 'I behaved ill to him, Aunt Rebecca. I was a very hardened young man.'

'Indeed, you were a very charming one, John, and always my favourite; so bright and kindly, and such a bonny boy. You are handsomer now, perhaps, but the fire has gone out of you.'

'I'm afraid it was wild-fire,' said the Colonel, gloomily. 'Where are these children?'

Aunt Rebecca fetched them in, and explained them, like a demonstrator in a museum. 'This is John, and this is Malcolm. John is the cleverer of the two; but Malcolm's a clinging sort of child, with such a sweet temper;' and so forth, as only an old maid can.

'Which is the elder?' inquired the Colonel.

'John is three weeks older,' replied the old lady. 'It's not much.'

'And then he's of the elder branch. That's as it should be; he shall have Grangehead, Aunt Rebecca.'

'Oh, do you think that's quite necessary?' she inquired, a little chopfallen, in the interest of the clinging child with the sweet temper. It was the first time she had crossed the Colonel's path. I may add it was the last. He was not angry; he had no wish to terrify the harmless lady; but when the man's spirit rose, as it always did at a thought of opposition, his voice rose along with it; and the mere volume of sound was appalling to the frail old dame.

'Primogeniture is the law of the land!' he bawled; 'and'—he was going to have added it was the law of God, but thought better of this flight. 'And a very good thing too,' he substituted. 'However, I don't bind myself; I shall test the children thoroughly.'

'I thought he was a soldier?' demanded John, in the tone of one who has paid for his seat and means to have his entertainment.

'So I am, little man,' said the Colonel.

'Where's your sword, then?'

'There's nobody here to fight with; nobody but kind aunties and good little boys. But you shall see my sword some of these days, and a case of pistols. Would you like to be a soldier?'

'That I would!' replied the child.

ROBERT LOUIS STEVENSON

'So you shall, I hope,' answered the Colonel, with emotion;
'one of Christ's soldiers.'

It was plain he had taken a fancy to John.

CHAPTER II

The whole party moved to Grangehead. It was a rambling old house, most of it only one story high, and none of it higher than two; it seemed to have been built at odd times, and it was difficult to tell where the mansion stopped and the offices began. The grounds were overgrown with hollies and laurels. In summer many fungi prospered in the thicket, and breathed out faint odours upon passers-by; but there were also many lilacs which beautified and perfumed the place in spring. A large paddock, almost large enough to justify the name of 'park' by which it went, was the playground of the two boys; there was besides a belfry over the gate of the stableyard, a great range of roof to clamber on, a draw-well under an old yew in a dark part of the shrubbery, and many other romantic accidents such as youth delights in. A broken-spirited tutor disposed of their mornings.

The Colonel himself was in his element. He accepted office as elder in the parish church, where his grand manners imparted a flavour of ritual to the boldest ceremonies of Scotch Presbyterianism. He was hand and glove with the subjected clergyman, and his big voice ruled in the Kirk Session. Once in a while, of a Saturday or Sunday evening, he would give a little lecture in the school-room; when he would now besiege the obdurate with denunciations, now delight the simple with soldierly anecdotes and barrack sentiment. It was a mystery to all how Colonel Falconer managed to be so blunt, and plain, and guileless, and simple-hearted as he did on these occasions; for, personally, he was quite a man of the world. He would even throw in a broad Scotch accent on an occasion. It was at these moments that cynical friends discussed the expression of his mouth. But the commonalty were vastly pleased. This man, who had imbued himself all over in the blood of persons of colour, and made a reputation in the army, proved, when put to the touch before a critical audience in the school-room of Grangehead, no great theologian after all, but a plain Christian who was most fitted to touch the hearts of children. That was somehow agreeable to all the hinds. It was concluded that the Colonel was a manly Christian; that was his variety in the local classification.

Poor old Miss Rebecca had been ordered up to Grangehead to help with the children. She soon withered; the Colonel rode her down, horse and van, so to speak. His iron nerves, his cruelly resounding voice, his abrupt decisions, the company and regimental devotions in which she had to take part under his eye—all these things preyed upon her like a disease. Colonel Falconer was her ideal; she had no fault to find with him. But she pined in his neighbourhood—a malady incident to maids—and passed away.

The Colonel was inconsolable; and thenceforward he was a little harsher to the boys. He had always been harsh, without ever being unkind, if you can understand that. The boys were not afraid of him in any deep sense, even loved him after a fashion; but they were shudderingly averse to his society. He was rude to them on principle; he made their lives as dull and bitter as he could, because he thought that was best for them, and he imagined he had so disenchanted existence, that there were no pleasures within their reach, except the pleasures of religion. He reckoned without boyhood, without the paddock, without the roof, without the draw-well in the shrubbery, without the fungi all summer under the laurels, without the sun, and winds, and seasons. The Colonel did his best; but it is easier to command any conceivable number of sepoys than to take the interest and poetry out of young people's lives.

John was a boy with what is called a deep nature—that is to say, he began to mature very early; wrote hymns and other performances, which he hid away in a confusion if anyone approached; was addicted to long meditation, and showed at times a morose and flighty character. Altogether, a boy to be looked after, with plenty of predisposition to evil, and all the passions impending. Malcolm was easy-going, and a little shallow; he had petty selfishnesses, for which John made way with rather a grand air; but then he could put his pride in his pocket to appease others, and had a winning way.

There never was any doubt but John should inherit. He was a boy after the Colonel's heart—proud, brave, gloomy, and with a natural talent for religion. Accordingly, he was affianced to Miss Mary Rolland, a girl of his own age, and heiress of the next estate. Mary and John understood their position; and they were always great friends. As soon as John was of age, they were to be married.

CHAPTER III

John was eighteen on the 12th of May, 18—. It was adorable weather. All the lilacs were in flower and all the birds were in love about the gardens of Grangehead; the wind smelt of spring. Mary Rolland and her father had dined with the Falconers, and the whole party strolled into the garden; for there was no loitering over wine at the Colonel's table.

'No, sir, I will not let that pass,' roared the host. 'It is a matter of principle; I will not bate an ace on it.'

'My dear sir,' replied Mr. Rolland, 'my very dear sir, pardon me for saying so, but, indeed, you take this rather warmly. I believe I may say I am a man of principle myself. I have never paltered or temporised; but I must make distinctions.'

'I make no distinctions,' answered the Colonel, 'in matters of principle. Is it a matter of principle, yes or no?'

'Christian liberty,' began Mr. Rolland.

'Don't let me hear the phrase,' interrupted the Colonel.

'I believe it is unimpeachably orthodox,' replied the other, somewhat nettled. 'I believe I could name authorities. Indeed, if I am not mistaken, it occurs in the Bible. Malcolm, will you fetch a testament?'

'It has been abused, Mr. Rolland. People have wrested it to their own damnation. Humble Christians should reverence it as a mystery; not bandy it about in disputations.' There was a flush under the curry-coloured cheek; the Colonel was on his war charger for the evening.

'Come away, Mary,' whispered John, pettishly. 'There'll be no end to this sort of thing.'

They went up a path among the evergreens, somewhat dark already, but closed at the far end by a piece of golden sky. The cover was musical on either side. Mary walked slowly, looking on the ground; John, who kept half a step in advance, could not keep his eyes from her. She seemed to have changed; there was more meaning, more life, more blood about her; from a pale, wiry slip of a girl, she had blossomed and spread, and become soft and rich, and foreign-looking. John was confused.

At the end of the path there was an open space with a seat, and a low parapet wall overlooking a public highway, and a great prospect of wood and meadow, bounded to the north by a range of hills. A river glittered along the plain in broken segments. The outline of the hills was bitten into the luminous sky. Clouds of birds passed to and fro between the clumps of plantation.

'Have you written any more poetry?' asked John.

'No.' She spoke in a constrained voice; it was a lie, and she lied clumsily, being still very young.

'You promised you would write something for my birthday.'

'I found I couldn't,' she said.

There was a pause. 'I am so glad we are going to be married,' he said, blankly. It elicited no answer, and she did not take her eyes off the distant view. John sighed. 'I am so fond of—of looking at sunsets,' he said. The speech came in two in the middle, and the end was patently not the proper sequel of the beginning.

'So am I,' she answered, with a sort of fervour.

'I wonder what has come over us. One would think we weren't happy,' he remarked.

'Oh! but I am happy.'

'So am I,' he said, in his turn, 'very happy—very happy;' and he repeated the words vacantly several times. They had never been sparing of caresses to each other, since their nurses had taught them to kiss; and so he was confounded when, on trying to take her hand, he found it withdrawn from him nervously. He waited abashed for some moments, and then he made a sort of effort, for he was frightened at the restraint and the disorder of his own feelings, and wished to do something which should break the spell and bring them back to natural terms of intercourse. He tried to kiss her. She sprang back in a commotion, turned white and red, and then white again, and stood a little way off, silent and seemingly indignant.

'She must hate me,' thought John. He was no great doctor in the schools of love; he was better up in the catechism, poor lad.

It was a relief to both when they heard Mr. Rolland calling for Mary, and they returned in silence to the lawn.

He walked so far home with them, on her father's invitation; and the old gentleman spoke with him very kindly by the way. Mary was quite silent; but her colour was a little heightened, and her eyes, which seemed no longer to avoid his gaze, looked very bright and soft.

Tall gates of iron, and an approach of lilacs, gave admission to Grangehead. The approach was buried in transparent shadow. A single blackbird fluted vaingloriously among the lilacs, a sweet smell of evening was abroad upon the air, the view was bounded by the sharp outline of the laurel thickets, and the gables of the house imprinted on the luminous west. Malcolm, with his head bent forward and his hands clasped behind his back, was pacing the gravel with slow, uneven footsteps. He affected not to hear John's approach, for he did not turn. But John overtook him, and in schoolboy fashion threw his arm about his neck. Malcolm shook him off.

'Leave me alone,' he said, testily.

'Why, what's wrong with you, Malcolm?' said John.

'I want to be alone.'

'Oh, by all means!' said John, and he passed him several steps in a fling of ruffled vanity. But he came to his better self in a moment. Malcolm was certainly moved beyond his custom, and it was not an occasion to be nice on points of etiquette, so John came back. 'Tell me what's wrong with you, Malcolm?' he repeated, 'there's a good lad! Tell me what's wrong?'

'I never said anything to you, did I?' returned the other in a flash. 'I can die, but I won't whine. You've got everything else—you've got the estate, and Mary, and everything—you may leave me my own company.'

John was dumbfounded.

'Malcolm, Malcolm,' he cried, 'you know very well that what's mine is yours. You know very well we're to share and share alike. Do you think I could be happy and leave you out? You know me better than that.'

'It's not the estate,' said Malcolm with a sob. 'It's the girl, man—it's the girl!' and he covered his face passionately with his hands.

John became grave. 'Do you love her?' he asked.

'Do I not!' replied the other, throwing up his arms with a wild gesture. 'Love her? Do I not!' He was very young.

A number of ugly thoughts presented themselves simultaneously at the door of John's mind. He suffered a furious spasm of the under lip. 'Does she love you?' he demanded.

'Do you think she loves you?' returned his cousin, with something like a sneer.

It was a Scotch answer, as people say in the North; but it sent John into the depths of despair. Everything was plain enough now; Mary hated him, as he had imagined. She loved Malcolm. They loved each other. In all likelihood there was an understanding between them. He was no more than an absurd and hateful obstacle in the lives of the two persons who were dearest to him.

Malcolm had made the answer in a tiff, and because he could say nothing more to the purpose. He had no reason to suppose Mary loved him. She seemed fond enough of his society, indeed; but then they usually conversed of John. He began to repent. 'It's not the estate,' he repeated, with a whimper; 'it's only Mary I mind; I can't live without her. But I can die,' he added, cheerfully.

'The two go together, my boy,' replied John. 'You must have both or neither—both or neither.' He shook his head mechanically for a long time. He was maturing a great scheme of self-sacrifice with hereditary gusto. The blood of wrong-headed old Covenanters, the blood of the Colonel was working darkly in his heart.

Suddenly a bell interrupted the stillness with a precipitate, undignified clangour. The blackbird flew away. It was the signal for family worship. John took Malcolm's hand solemnly.

'Malcolm,' he said, 'we are nearer than most brothers. I'll do all I can for you.'

CHAPTER IV

Family worship at Grangehead was an affair of great precision. All the servants were expected to attend, morning and evening. The Colonel read aloud a chapter from the Old Testament and one from the New, and delivered a long prayer extempore. His voice was loud and hurried, as if he was calling a roll before proceeding to business; and of course the servants never listened. When the prayer was over, breakfast began in the morning; and at night everyone was expected to retire. On the evening of his birthday John requested a private interview with his uncle.

The Colonel looked at him sharply, and then bade him follow him to the study, where he took a chair himself, and motioned his nephew to another. But John preferred to stand.

'Well, what is it?'

'I understand, Sir,' began John, 'that I am to succeed you in the property; and I wished—'

'I don't choose to discuss these matters,' said the Colonel; 'above all, with you. In the meantime you are one of my nephews, and no more. Is that all?'

'Indeed, Sir, you do not understand me. You must allow me to explain. It is a matter of conscience.'

'Oh, if it's a matter of conscience!' said the Colonel; and he made an urbane movement with his hand.

'Malcolm is in love with Mary, Sir,' said John.

'Well?' bawled the Colonel.

'He cannot marry her unless he is to have the property,' continued John; 'and for my part I would rather not have it. I would far sooner make a way in the world for myself. I wish to be independent, and owe everything to my own spirit; and there is no fear of me. I could be a clergyman and save souls, or a soldier like you, or go to a colony; there is no fear of that. And think, Sir, what it would be for poor Malcolm to lose all he cares about in the world; and for me, if I had taken it all away from him!'

'I thought you liked the girl yourself,' said the Colonel.

'I do.' John's mouth was very dry.

The Colonel jumped up and shook John by the hand.

'You're a fine fellow, Sir,' he cried. 'I honour you for every word you've said. You're a nephew after my own heart, and I believe after God's. But as to what you say, of course it's nonsense. I leave the property to please myself and for God's glory, and for neither your pleasure nor Malcolm's; and you must take it, as I took it, as a talent. Yes, lad,' he added, 'that's the word that will make it all come easily to you. A talent—perhaps a cross. Bear it for His sake.' And he brought his hand down upon John's shoulder with kindly violence.

'But Malcolm,' began John.

'Go to bed,' cried the Colonel. 'I forgive you, but I'll hear no more of it. And mind you pray against spiritual pride. I know you; you're a fine lad; but there lies your stumbling-block. You wish to play the martyr.' People will spy their own foibles through chain-mail.

Of course John was bitterly indignant. All this praise rankled in his conscience, and made him suspicious of his own sincerity. If it were only to reinstate his self-respect, he must consummate the sacrifice. Moreover, the Colonel's last insinuation was too near the truth not to be galling. But he dared not struggle further, and said 'Good night,' leaving the Colonel to thank God upon his knees for his nephew's excellence.

An Old Song

In his own room he threw the window open, and sat down to nurse his desperate determination. The flush had died out of the west; the night was full of stars; troops of dark trees huddled together in the twilight and rocked in faint airs. From the stable court he could hear the watch-dog jangle his chain, or a wakeful horse moving in the stall. He contemplated the stars with imbecility. Sometimes he walked about the room; sometimes he sat down again and began eloquent letters; often he fell bitterly to prayer. The whole subject had gone beyond his control into the region of the imagination, where it worked and fermented, and cast up a fine froth of mock heroics. He would make everybody else happy, and be himself supremely miserable. They should wallow in luxuries; he would live on dry bread in a garret. If he made enough for superfluity, it should be forwarded secretly to add some infinitesimal detail to their felicity. Sometimes a pale face would be seen in the shrubbery; the children would flee from it with screams, while the unknown benefactor made his escape unnoticed. At last he would die on a pallet; everybody would troop around him with tears and apologies, and his grave would be daily visited by those whom he had served.

This sort of fanfaronade was often interrupted by transports of genuine feeling. The boy's love for Mary had roots in his soul, and at times he was beside himself at the thought of losing her.

About three in the morning, as he was leaning out of the window, a train passed many miles off under the range of hills. Just before the sound of its passage died out of earshot, the long shrill scream of the whistle ascended towards the stars. I wonder whether people who were young in the days of stage-coaches and guards'-horns, know what a trouble is brought into the minds of wakeful youth by the sound of a railway whistle. A lad is shown all the kingdoms of the earth in a vision; and, although he is eminently happy where he is, with loving friends and a half-written poem in his desk, he positively despises himself because he is not going somewhere else. You may imagine what it was to John. Thank God! he had the world before him; he would begin anew, and carve out something noble for a career.

He dozed a little in a chair, and was wakened by horrible dreams. His ears were filled with Babel; he was thrust hither and thither in a crowd of vile spectres, and heard the Colonel calling upon him from an incalculable distance. When he awoke, the light of the candle dazzled and distressed him, and he was afraid of the shadows.

Some time before sunrise he suddenly burst out bleeding at the nose, and had hard ado to get it staunched. He soaked his clothes by holding a wet sponge to the nape of his neck, and the coolness gratified so much that he took a bath. This seemed to clear his head and steady his nerves; the more acute symptoms of fever passed away; and he slipped out into the garden in the dawn, with something like composure in his heart.

He walked for a while in the approach, and made some very impassioned verses to Mary, to Malcolm, to his own heart, to God for strength, to the sunrise; all of which he forgot as soon as he had made them, although that was no great matter. He went and sat on the parapet where he had been last night with Mary. The stones were wet with dew; mists were scattered on the plain; there was a great lowing of cattle and bleating of sheep; women with pails and whistling plough-lads began to go by underneath him on the public road. Here he prayed very heartily, wept a good deal, and, for two moments, was near giving up his intention. But the bell for prayers cut in upon this mood, played havoc with his disordered nerves, and called back the dark perversity upon his soul. The harm that is done by ugly bells ill-rung is not to be computed.

CHAPTER V

At breakfast John ate nothing, and drank a great deal of strong tea, which was very bad for him. There never was much talk at this meal, except on Sundays; during the week the Colonel had the papers to read, and a considerable correspondence besides, and the cousins usually brought a book to table. But on this particular morning the Colonel went twice out of his way to address an agreeable remark to John, and looked at him covertly from time to time with much affection; for he had been thinking his nephew over, and was vastly pleased with him. John answered roughly and sourly. The idea of speaking pleasantly over a break-fast-table to a hero and a martyr!

The cover was removed, and John was pretending to read the newspaper over the fire, when his uncle returned with a letter in his hand. He had a very kind look in his eyes as he spoke.

'Take this letter to Hutton, please' (Hutton was Mr. Rolland's place), 'and wait an answer.'

It was now the moment for action. John drew himself together with a great effort; he did not raise his head from the paper.

'Thank you,' he answered, quietly, 'I prefer staying where I am.'

If a thunderbolt had fallen upon Grangehead, it would have discomposed the Colonel less. John could see him over the edge of the paper. He stood quite still, but the immovable eyebrows went up, and his whole face underwent a swift and rather ghastly change. He seemed about to speak, but he thought better of it, went to the window, and looked out for perhaps a minute and a half. Then he turned to John and addressed him once more.

'I am not sure whether you heard me. I desired you to take this letter to Hutton. I am not in the habit of repeating my commands.' Thus far he spoke firmly, and in his usual loud voice; but there he seemed to take fright, and added hurriedly, and in an unsteady tone, 'You can take a horse, if you like, John.'

Even John, full as he was of heroic and satanic humours, was shocked at his uncle's condescension; his heart yearned to him, and he longed to throw himself on his knees and avow all. It is so hard to insult a person you have respected all your life! But the devil was uppermost.

'I think I said I should prefer to remain where I am,' he answered.

'Oh, very well,' said the Colonel; and he left the room.

John had expected a blow. He was frightened and elated at the turn affairs had taken, and prayed fervently.

In the meantime Malcolm had repented of last night's scene, in which he felt he had played a childish and perhaps a questionably honest part; and he desired heartily to make it up to John in kindness. He came into the dining-room with a penitent but cheerful spirit, and took a seat on the opposite side of the hearth.

'About Mary—,' he began.

'Hold your tongue!' returned John. It was a discharge of nervous force, purely involuntary, and directed at no one in particular. The moment it had taken place he felt relieved, and sought to remove the effect. 'I beg your pardon, I did not hear what you were saying; I'm a little out of sorts this morning,' he explained.

Malcolm stared.

'It was only about Mary and what we said last night,' he continued.

'I shall see that you are happy,' replied the other, grandly. 'Make yourself easy. You have appealed to me, and it is now my business.'

'You needn't take it quite so high,' said Malcolm. 'I'm very much obliged to you, of course; but it's my business too, and I mean to explain—'

'I'm not in the humour for explanations,' interrupted John. 'I'll say my say if I choose.'

'You'll say it to yourself then.' And John rose.

'John,' said Malcolm, 'I beg your pardon if I spoke rudely. Indeed, I didn't mean. And I really do wish a word with you.'

'You may leave me my own company,' answered John, mimicking his cousin's voice.

'Oh, well, you may go and be blanked, for me!' flashed Malcolm. 'You're a blanked civil fellow, indeed! I wish you were dead!'

'I wouldn't swear if I were you, young man,' observed John.

Malcolm flung out of the room in a fine temper, and John heard him slamming doors all about the house, until a stentorian summons and a rumble of reprimand from the Colonel's study re-established peace. John felt very strangely. Thank God, he had quarrelled with everybody now! He was on the high seas of martyrdom. Malcolm was to be happy, thanks to him; and no one would suspect his heroism. I think he positively hated Malcolm; he would almost as soon have sought him out and strangled him, as gone on with the sacrifice that was to make him happy. His brain was in a whirl. He took a road on chance, and walked furiously. The trees danced on either side; the world reeled. Sometimes he was so dazzled he could see nothing; again, a corner of the road stood out before him in a sort of sickly distinctness; it seemed to mean something; it had something to do with his trouble, and he stared at it and hated it. The poor lad was in a fever.

In the course of this aimless walk he hit upon the county town, and, being consumed with thirst, he entered the hotel. The commercial room was occupied by a single personage—a pallid, red-haired, fat young bagman, seated by the fire, with a long tumbler of some beverage at his elbow. John sat as far away from him as he could, picked up a railway time-table, and turned over the pages without seeing a word. When the waiter came for his order, he pointed silently to the bagman's glass.

'Same as that gentleman, Sir? Yes, Sir,' said the waiter.

Now it happened for John's sins that the drink he had thus innocently commanded is one of the most insinuating mixtures in the world. Gin and gingerbeer, neither of them remarkable by themselves, become when mixed not only very agreeable, but exceptionally intoxicating. John was mightily pleased; his throat tingled, his brain cleared; the names of stations in the time-table became suddenly legible, and he gave himself over to a confused sort of luxury, picturing what sort of places these should be, and how the penniless martyr, John Falconer, should visit them one after another, and meet with singular adventures by the way. I think, as he got on with the second glass, there were even beautiful faces taking part in these adventures. For not only his love for Malcolm, but his love for Mary also, had suffered from the rivalry of Black Happiness and the violent dislocation of his hopes and prospects.

He did not reach Grangehead until the bell was ringing for dinner. He was aware of a distressing heat in his face, a noise in his ears, and a blur before his eyes. He had eaten nothing all day, had drunk more than was good for him, and still suffered from an unquenchable thirst. He took his place at table, dusty and disordered as he was; and his first action was to fill his glass with sherry and drink it off. The taste offended him, and he felt his head ache dully as he swallowed it; but he was too inexperienced to understand that he was getting drunk; he only knew that he was very ill, which was quite as it ought to be, and would bring on the reconciliation scene beside the pallet all the sooner.

The Colonel never addressed him. Malcolm, who felt that John was in disgrace, but attributed it merely to his unparalleled conduct in not coming home to luncheon, was also a little shy of speaking to him. As for their tiff in the morning, Malcolm had long ago forgiven that.

Towards the end of dinner the sherry began to operate, and John took the lead in the conversation.

'This is a hateful place—Grangehead,' he volunteered, cheerfully.

The Colonel looked at him sharply.

'There's no life,' he continued; 'no v'riety. Young men should see th' world.'

Malcolm was alarmed, and telegraphed to him to be silent; but he could not understand the hint, or, if he did, resented it. The Colonel listened with growing attention: the wind was rising in that quarter.

'It's not good, whatever you may think,' John proceeded, 'for young men of tal'nt to be shut up with 'n old man, whoever he is.'

He poured sherry into his tumbler and drank it off. He then looked at the empty tumbler with a maudlin laugh.

''T occurs to me,' he began, '—'t occurs to me—.' And he stopped and smiled.

'It occurs to me, Sir,' bawled the Colonel, 'that you're the worse of drink.'

John contemplated his uncle in a vacillating way.

'Tha' 's a lie,' he remarked; and then, repeating it with a giggle, as if he had said rather a good thing, 'Tha' 's a lie,' said he, 'tha' 's a lie.'

Malcolm and the Colonel rose at the same moment, the former with some idea of interference. The Colonel whipped John out of his chair, and swept him irresistibly to the front door. Three stone steps, with a bit of iron railing on either hand, joined the level of the gravel plot to the level of the entrance hall. Standing on the top of these, the Colonel gave his nephew so smart an impulsion that he descended the stairs at one step, alighted on his left foot, fell thence on his right knee, and finally sprawled at full length upon the gravel.

'Let me see no more of you,' shouted the Colonel. 'I bar my door against you for ever. I am done with you for time and eternity. God forgive you as I do;' and all unconscious of the irony of his last prayer, he re-entered the house, and shut the door.

John lay as he had fallen in a stupor. Meantime, the sun began to turn the west into a lake of gold, and the blackbird sang among the lilacs as before.

CHAPTER VI

Malcolm was left alone in the dining-room in a pitiful situation. He could understand from such sounds as reached him that John had been turned bodily out of doors, and that the Colonel had retired to brood in his private room. Grangehead and Mary were both his own, and yet I assure you he gave neither of them one thought. His mind was full of his cousin, and what could be done to bring about a reconciliation. He finished his wine mechanically. An hour went over his head, and he was still drawing patterns on the plate before him, when an alarmed servant peeped in, and asked if she might take away the things. This shook him into a resolution, and he went straight to his uncle. You must remember that Malcolm had never been the favourite nephew, and even when all went well, would have thought twice before he ventured on a similar intrusion.

The Colonel had neglected to turn up his reading-lamp on entering, so that the room was in twilight and filled with large shadows. He sat at the table, with his head on his hand and his face wholly shaded; even when Malcolm entered and addressed him, he gave no sign of life.

'Sir,' said Malcolm, 'I trust there is nothing serious between you and John.'

'My dear boy,' returned the Colonel, with his hand still over his brow, 'I have been expecting you; you may spare me the rest of your expostulations, which I can very well imagine for myself.

You have mentioned the name of a person whom I once loved, but between him and me, there is an end of everything. I am a sinful man, perhaps a hard one; at least I did my best to be kind to him. But now he has provoked me beyond the power of God to make me forgive him, and I blot him out of my memory for ever. You see how it is,' he resumed, after a moment's pause. 'Out of consideration for yourself and out of respect for me, you will have to avoid this subject in the future. And remember, you must try and humour me now, for you are all I have left.'

He motioned him away, and Malcolm durst not hesitate. As he closed the door he thought he overheard the sound of a groan; and this impressed and terrified him more than ever. He sat on the stairs with his head in his hands, and tried to think. But he could make nothing of it; the pillars of the earth were moved, natural laws were all suspended. The human mind cannot change its base of operations fast enough for certain sweeping catastrophes.

He rose at last and cautiously opened the front door. It was getting very dark; but he could see something darker on the gravel. It lay so still that his heart began to misgive him dreadfully, and he stole down the steps and nearer to the body. He could hear stertorous breathing, now and then rising into a snore, and breaking off again; and as his alarm was quieted, its place was taken by contempt and some disgust.

As he returned to the house, Grangehead and Mary had become at least agreeable features in the background. He was getting reconciled to the new order of things, and sought rather to improve than to alter it. Out of his own savings and those of John (for they kept their money together) he made a purse of about thirty pounds. This he put into one pocket of a large, warm driving-coat, balancing it in the other with John's Bible. And thus equipped he returned to the figure on the gravel.

'John!' he said; 'John!'

John answered with a snort. Every fibre of Malcolm's Puritanical body shuddered in revolt; and throwing the coat over his cousin, he fled back into the house.

There never was a night like that a Grangehead. There was no tea and no family worship. Mr. John slept on the gravel; Mr. Malcolm slept by the dining-room fire; and the Colonel sat up in his own room in meditation and religious exercise.

CHAPTER VII

The Colonel hung his head from that day forward. He turned suddenly and surprisingly bald; his face seemed to have shrunken and fallen in; and there were broken tones in his voice. Malcolm never uttered John's name in his uncle's presence; but he thought of him often enough as he looked upon these changes. The old man had been stabbed to the heart—slower or faster, he was dying.

There could be no doubt that he kept himself acquainted with John's life, and would have grasped at any excuse to make up the difference and get his favourite nephew home again. But John's conduct was of a nature to pain the Colonel deeply; every bulletin must have been another cowardly blow on his white head; and though he assisted his nephew underhand, neither his pride nor his principle would allow him to kill the fatted calf for such an unregenerate prodigal.

The end came, when the two lads were in their twenty-first year—John writing leader notes in a London newspaper, and Malcolm agreeably conscious of his approaching marriage with Mary Rolland. The Colonel took to bed rather suddenly. It was wild, windy weather, and the sky was full of flying vapours. He had been looking out of the window all the afternoon, and towards dusk he called Malcolm and pointed to the labouring trees and the dead leaves whirling in the open.

'I'm too old and tired for this sort of thing,' he said; 'I think

I'll go to bed.' He l[...]
up again,' he adde[...]
illness he complain[...]
weather continued [...]
of sailors, and be [...]
and land.

At last one a[...]
prop him up wit[...]

'I put it off, a[...]
afraid I put it off [...]

Malcolm set [...]

'Here is the [...]

'It's the last [...]

Malcolm's face wa[s]
known the Colonel[...]
mood, and rende[...]
confessing pre[...]
past.
'No[...]
too go[...]

the key with a smile. 'It's strange, strange to think o.. [...]
gust howled in the chimney, and the house quaked. 'I wish I could be spared this wind; nevertheless, not my will, but Thine! I'm as full of fancies as a girl,' he added, opening the box. 'It's a poor account of an old soldier, Malcolm; but we all show the white feather towards the end; the lamp burns low, you see, and the blood runs cold. I've been in sharp affairs in my day, both on sea and land, and many a time I thought I had come to my last hour; but I never knew our need of a Divine Helper until now. I don't mind a stand-up fight; but this lying here in the dark brings a man to his marrow-bones.' He had been turning over the papers during these last words, and now produced a sealed envelope. 'Aye, here it is,' he went on. 'And now, Malcolm, mark what I say. I don't wish to open up old sores. I once thought of telling you the story; but it would do no good, and things are best as they are. So I take this way. What is in this envelope refers to—to one whom I have not mentioned for some years. I wish you to know that I loved that person as if he had been my own son, born out of my loins. Yet I was hard on him—very hard, and I pray God's forgiveness.'

streaming with tears. All the time he had
stern and gloomy, merely set off his present
red it more touching. The bystander, besides
sent sympathy, accused himself of injustice in the

uncle,' he cried, 'you never were hard; you were only
od.'

'Hush!' said the old man. 'This is no time for flattery. I am
going where I shall hear the truth plump and plain. I was a hard,
proud man; I was hard on my father, I was hard on you, and I was
very hard on him. If ever a man needed the merits of Another,
here he lies, Malcolm—here he lies. And now, when you see John,
you're to tell him that I forgave him, and asked his forgiveness.
Don't forget the last. And if ever you should be tempted to
quarrel with him, or if ever you have it in your power to do him
a service and hesitate to do it, or if ever he does you an injury that
you can't forgive, open this envelope, read the letter twice over—
twice, mark you—and then down on your knees before your
Maker for His guiding Spirit. And remember this, I've tried
being a hard man, and you see the kind of death-bed it has brought
me to; be you easy, Malcolm—mind and be you easy!'

He stopped exhausted, for he had been speaking with some
vehemence.

'But how should I quarrel with John?' asked Malcolm; 'or
why should he do me an injury?'

'I don't very well know; but circumstances are a great thing,'
answered the Colonel, philosophically.

'Uncle,' objected Malcolm, 'you are putting a secret into my
life. Let me open the envelope at once, or as soon as—I mean—'

'As soon as I am dead!' the Colonel continued for him. 'I have
told you already when you may open it, and I don't go back from
my word. These are my orders, Sir. I always was a peremptory
man; of course I know little or nothing about a future state, and

speak under correction; but I rather suspect I shall be a very peremptory spirit.' This with a grim smile. 'Now you understand. Take away the box, and leave me alone for awhile, like a good fellow.'

In the course of the week the old man's mind began to wander. He commanded Sepoy regiments with great pluck, and addressed meetings in the school-room on religious topics. He talked much about John; and sometimes returned on the escapades of his own wild youth in a manner that profoundly afflicted and humiliated Malcolm as he watched alone by the bed. Towards the end he was clearer and very composed, said good-bye to everyone about the house, warning them against hardness and pride; and finally surrendered his sword between six and seven o'clock of a black, tempestuous evening, amidst the genuine grief of many who had only feared him while alive.

Malcolm stood over the fire that same night with the sealed envelope in his hand; now he was in a mind to burn it, and be done with all uncertainty; now he had his finger under the flap to tear it open. But it was an act of disloyalty to the dead, from which his sense of honour recoiled. Nor was this sentiment unhelped by circumstances. The candles winked and flickered in the draughts, and peopled the room with moving shadows, which seemed to spy upon him from behind; and the noise of the winds raving round the house in the darkness, chilled his blood and inclined him to superstitious terrors. He did not really imagine that the spirit of the dead Colonel on his Indian war-horse came charging up the approach with every gust; but somehow it struck him as not being a nice sort of evening for the business. And so he put the envelope into a casket by itself, locked it, and, venturing forth in all this uproar of the elements, threw the key into the draw-well in the shrubbery.

He felt relieved that very moment. The truth is, he had a shrewd guess of what the secret was, and dreaded nervously to learn that he was right. For some days longer the uncertainty haunted him; but by the end of a month he had practically lived it down, and before he had made all ready for the reception of his wife, the idea only recurred to him as a passing curiosity when he had nothing else to think about.

CHAPTER VIII

At first John had to swim very hard for existence; indeed, I scarcely understand how he kept his head above water at all. But he made friends, and the friends got him on to a newspaper in some subaltern capacity. When that newspaper failed, he found another more readily; and thus, like a man walking on a hill-side where every foothold breaks away as he quits it, he went on from journal to journal, as one after another silently expired. I don't think he ever was connected with one that kept alive above a year.

He had written a large volume of poetry about himself and Mary Rolland and Malcolm, in delicately veiled allusion. I am told it scanned very well, and contained quite a surprising number of invocations to the Deity, and, comparatively speaking, no punctuation. And yet somehow it went against the heart of the publishing interest, and remained in manuscript. John took to being rather cynical and worldly, sneered at poetry, and dare-say'd, over public-house tables, that he would turn his attention to politics one of these days, and change the face of Europe.

He lived from hand to mouth; and the hand was not always spotless, which fostered his cynicism. To a man in an abject situation, a good twanging snarl is a sort of moral pinch of snuff, and pulls his nerves together. From quite an early period he looked back with some contempt upon the episode of his departure. The hollow parts of it, the swollen vanity, were apparent at a glance; and he used to laugh at himself, not quite heartily perhaps, when he fell thinking of old days. I don't think the laugh was quite genuine, because he very often had a glass of something after one of these attacks of solitary merriment. But then, of course, wine and laughter go together by rights.

He heard with sincere affliction of his uncle's death. A little while after, and the news of Malcolm's marriage followed. He was in great form that evening, and made some capital hits—above all, when he 'stood' the company all round, and in a little humorous speech explained this unusual prodigality. His aunt had died, and in spite of the machinations of his wicked cousin, he was about to lead to the altar a young lady of remarkable attractions and great wealth. He made everybody die with laughing as he described this heroine, and expatiated on his own transports; and when it was done he laughed a very great deal over it himself, although he had preserved his gravity inimitably throughout. So you see John was quite a gay young fellow when he was twenty-one.

When he was well on in his thirties, another newspaper foundered under his feet. He was a confirmed prodigal, and when the pay stopped had not a halfpenny to call his own. He walked home through the Park, with his hands in his pockets, very glad to think that he had no longer any obligation to produce copy, and not much concerned about his empty purse, for he had the true Bohemian feeling—I don't know whether to call it an incredulity or a faith—about money. He got into conversation with some children (he was always fond of the young); through them he scraped acquaintance with the nurserymaid; then he fell in tow with an old man covered with sham jewellery, who whiled away some time in a very humorous manner; and finally night began to overtake him without much prospect of dinner. Like the prodigal son, he began to reflect upon his circumstances; and suddenly a thought occurred to him, and he exclaimed, with a laugh, 'Egad, I'll go visit my cousins in the country.'

He made up his kit in the course of the next day, and borrowed some money among his penniless acquaintance. It was not enough to carry him to his journey's end, and he accomplished the last score of miles on foot. He was weary, and it was already dark when he reached the iron gate and the approach of lilacs. He drew near the house with more emotion than he had anticipated; his heart beat painfully; and after he had pulled the bell he felt inclined to run away.

Malcolm and his wife were sitting over the fire. She was about some needlework, and he had just given vent to a portentous yawn, when the servant brought in a soiled visiting card.

'Mr. John Falconer,' read Malcolm. 'God bless me!'

'Of all places in the world,' cried Mary, 'what should bring him here?'

'We must see him, of course,' observed the husband.

'It is most annoying—after so many years!' said the wife.

'Show Mr. Falconer in.'

He was not going to be welcomed with much warmth, it would appear. The fact is, both Malcolm and Mary had reasons of their own. On his part, John was recuperating his cynicism on the doorstep; and when he was asked to follow the servant, instead of seeing his cousin come towards him with open arms, he felt as if a leading article were too good for mankind.

When he came to the door of the room, he stopped with a painful impression. The room and the two people seemed unchanged. A gush of regret and love came over him in a moment, and all his hard thoughts melted and disappeared. Nor was he more struck with their unchanged looks than they with the pitiful alteration that had overtaken him in his knotless and arduous existence. They had been preserved in a bottle of Domestic Spirits; he had been blown about with all winds. He was bald, haggard, and lean. And when he dashed forward and caught each of them by a hand, and cried, 'Malcolm!—Mary!—Malcolm!' their hearts thawed towards him, and they wrung him by the hand, and made as much of him as if they had been longing for his return.

'My uncle's dead?' he asked, suddenly, as if he had heard some rumour, but desired corroboration.

'Eighteen years ago last winter,' answered Malcolm. 'He died asking your forgiveness.'

'Eighteen—eighteen years ago!' John repeated. 'And my forgiveness! Why, God help us all, is that not strange?'

He looked so dazed and half-crazy that Malcolm tried to alter the tenor of his thoughts; but he stuck to his point.

'He must have been changed,' he said; 'greatly changed. I would give my hand off, now, to have seen him before he died. He was a grand old man, our uncle, Colonel Falconer; God rest his soul, he was a grand old man! And yourselves,' he added, with a sudden and most engaging change of manner; 'tell me how happy you are, and exaggerate if you can. You know you're the only two old friends that I possess in this big world. Tell me about the children, Mary!'

It was long past twelve before Mary retired, and nearer four than three when her lord followed her. And the next day John was domesticated at Grangehead; no one would listen to any talk of limitation; here was a family which had been scattered by an unkind fate, and was now happily reunited.

CHAPTER IX

There was plenty for John to do. Among these quite idle people another idler seemed rather a busy personage. He addicted himself, from constitutional considerations, to gardening—gardening being taken in its usual amateur sense of digging potatoes for ten minutes in the forenoon, and hanging round all the evening with a straw hat and a watering-pot. He recommended a course of reading for the oldest boy, comprising some slashing Radical works which took Malcolm's breath away. And with the young children he was always charming. He would sit on a garden seat the whole summer day, smoking a clay pipe and telling them stories; every now and then it would be, 'Run away and give Jane my very respectful compliments, and ask her to be so very polite as send me out a glass of beer.'

He had many perplexing ways. It was impossible to guess when he might go to bed or when he might rise. He could not be trusted with the slightest message; he would sometimes insult visitors on controversial topics; and he firmly refused to go to church, which made a great scandal throughout the parish. The most charitable verdict was one by an emphatic middle-aged maiden lady, who had read all sorts of books, from 'Erechtheus' to 'Lothair', and so acquired a second-hand acquaintance with life. 'He is quite a literary man, my dear,' she explained. 'They are generally rather French in their habits.'

In the meanwhile a great revolution was happening in John's

mind. He no longer looked back with a sneer upon his own heroics: he took them in deadly earnest; he shunned the parapet wall where he had sat with Mary; he had dark, fitful humours, and affected long and solitary walks. Malcolm was sorry to remark these symptoms; poor John was so eccentric!

One day a careless servant let the rope fall into the draw-well. John had always liked clambering and start fits of exercise; he descended the well, and came up with the rope sure enough, but also with a little key sorely rusted. By the look of it, it must have lain for many years on the ledge where his hand had encountered it. Malcolm and he were alone in that cool, damp corner under the laurels and the yew; at the end of a path some way off they could see the sun lying bright and solid on the open; and this increased their grateful sense of shadow.

Malcolm was upset when John showed him the key. 'This is a very extraordinary providence,' he said, with some solemnity; 'this key has not reappeared for nothing. I threw it down on purpose.'

'Let us throw it in again,' answered John; and he was preparing to suit the action to the words, when Malcolm caught his arm.

'No, no; give it me!' he said. 'Since it has come back, God's will be done.'

'I say,' said John, sitting down on the edge of the well and folding his arms, 'this won't do. It's true you have a tendency to pious ejaculation, a substitute for a trick you used to have in old days. But that particular form means business. It means "here's something I don't like at any possible price, and I decline dealing." It means "God's will be done, and in the meantime I'll do all I can to see that it isn't." It means as near as may be "damn it!" Explain yourself.'

'John, John! I'm afraid you've lost all your religion.'

'Why, as to that, I'm rather afraid I have. But I'm after the key just now. Is it the key of Bluebeard's cellar, or of the subterranean passage which connects this ruinous pile with the sea-coast? You're looking down in the mouth, man. Throw it into the well, and defy augury.'

'I feel down in the mouth,' answered Malcolm. 'John,' he added, lowering his voice, 'do you believe in special providences?'

'Certainly not,' answered John.

'Well, I sometimes do, and this—mark my words—this is one.'

'This? Which?' demanded John; 'the key, or the well? or—or me, perhaps? Am I a special providence? I've been a special corre-spondent often enough.'

'The whole occurrence,' answered Malcolm; 'the—the cir-cumstance. It is providential, John, and it means mischief.'

'As far as I can find out,' replied the other, 'providence gener-ally does.'

'That is the kind of talk that a man repents when he comes to die,' observed Malcolm, sententiously.

'I didn't mean to shock you. It was merely a criticism of how people use their words. As for the subject itself, I decline jurisdic-tion. I know nothing of it, and care about as much.'

'You don't believe in a providence at all, I fancy.'

'My God! how can I—with my life?' asked John.

'I can—with mine,' returned Malcolm, rosily.

John sneered.

'I have no doubt I could do so too,' said he, 'if I had plenty of money and a wife and a litter of children. But then, you see, I haven't.'

'I suppose you might have had them if you'd chosen,' an-swered Malcolm, pettishly.

'Well, do you know, I rather suppose I might,' said John; and he stared the other strangely between the eyes.

'I shall never understand you, John.'

'I don't suppose you ever will.'

And the pair separated; Malcolm went into the house with the key, and it was John's hour for gardening.

CHAPTER X

Mary was an admirable Woman, and all that. At the same time she was not altogether a fool. She used to make poetry with John in the days of their engagement; since then she had read the History of England (which is more than the reader can say), a cookery book, a work on crochet, a vast quantity of novels and newspapers, and 'How I Found Livingstone', by Mr. Stanley. In fact, she was quite literary in her tastes. She had a strong, good head, a quiet and perfectly inflexible character, and no knowledge of the world. She was almost entirely engrossed by maternity; her husband had become the father of her children.

John she regarded somewhat in the light of an under-nursery-maid, who was also a pleasant companion for herself. She unmercifully abused his good-will, and never imagined that she was not conferring favours.

One day she and John were taking care of the two youngest at that seat beside the parapet which John was so careful to avoid when he was alone. Mary settled herself luxuriously in one corner and got her work ready.

'Now, if we had a book, you might read to me; that would be nice,' she said.

'Shall I fetch one?' he asked.

'Oh, no; never mind. We can talk, and that'll do just as well. Charlie, come back; do you hear me? There's that wretched child on the parapet, John; do take him away.'

'I came here the morning I left Grangehead, for ever, as I thought,' said John, returning to his seat. 'It was before dawn, and you couldn't see much across the road; it was like looking into my future. And I made a great many good resolutions, nearly all of which I have broken.'

'How very like you!' she said.

'Isn't it?'

'And what were they all about?'

'A great many things. I was never to return to Grangehead for one.'

'I'm glad you've broken that!'

'I was always to be sober and say my prayers, for another.'

'I'm afraid you've broken that, too.'

'And then I was never to love anyone but you,' he went on.

'Oh, oh!' she said, 'and that was the first to go!'

'I have never said so,' he answered. 'I never said I had broken them all.' She stole a glance at him; he was looking straight before him on the ground.

'I've dropped my worsted!' she said. 'How stupid! Will you pick it up? Thanks.'

John was a little huffed; he sat and brooded, while Mary talked easily of this or that, teething or measles, the doctor's wife or the clergyman's maiden sister.

'The clergyman's an ass,' broke in John.

'How do you know, when you never go to hear him?'

'Didn't he dine here? And the doctor, too? He's another ass.'

'Do you think we are all asses, then—we people in the country?' she asked.

'All but you, upon my word.'

'And Malcolm?'

'Malcolm? Oh, Malcolm's a different thing. I was an ass myself, as long as I lived here; and I've carried the panniers ever since in consequence. It's a poor thing to start in life with empty pockets and a broken heart! Ah, Mary! you don't know what a business it is to leave all that you love in the world and go out among strangers. Do you remember'—he had grown warm now —'do you remember the last evening we were here? It was such a beautiful evening! I thought you hated me, and it decided my life.'

She smiled. He had been banished Grangehead for insulting the Colonel while drunk; that was what had decided his life.

'You were a very silly fellow,' she said. 'Why was I to hate you? I never hated anybody, far less an old friend like you.'

'You hadn't written some verses for my birthday, as you promised. And—and you wouldn't let me kiss you.'

'I have no doubt I was quite right,' she said, decisively. 'May I trouble you to look after Charlie? he is on the wall again. And, oh! I think I will ask you to fetch a book; it will be so nice to be read to.'

She was alarmed and angry; even through her treble armour of innocence, pride, and selfishness she became aware that this man still loved her. It was insulting, it was cruel of him to refer to the time of their engagement. And in such a way, too! It was an indignity—it was almost a disgrace. She felt hot all over. 'I wish,' she exclaimed, fervently, 'I wish he had never come back. How are we ever to get rid of him without a scene?'

As John was coming back with the book, he met her rustling down the alley in great pomp, with a child in each hand. She had changed her mind; she would go into the house and rest; and she dismissed him with a queenly inclination.

John was furious; he went away and walked. By a sort of instinct he took the same road as on a former occasion, and found himself at the county town. He dined at the inn, and spent the evening in a corner of the smoking-room, drinking and sneering to himself at the conversation of the other guests. On one occasion he interfered with a few pleasant words, which nearly brought about a fight. The quarrel was adjusted after a fashion, and somewhat as spilt wine is covered with a napkin; he refused to apologise, and the whole company turned their backs on him. He was vastly pleased at this, and redoubled his cynicism.

It was quite late when he got home; the servants had gone to bed, and Malcolm opened the door himself. John, with his hands in his trousers pockets, regarded him offensively, as he put up the chain and shot the bolts.

'You are late,' said Malcolm, quietly.

But John only made answer with an affected laugh, and went away upstairs without salutation.

CHAPTER XI

The next morning it rained heavily. John was later than usual; and while he was sitting alone over breakfast, Malcolm came in and took a chair. He seemed embarrassed.

'My dear John,' he began, 'if I say anything on the subject, you will believe it is entirely for your own good; but last night I could not help thinking—'

'My dear Malcolm,' interrupted John, 'I had had a glass. Why, why beat about the bush?'

'You admit it; I am glad of that. Now, do allow me to say one word. You should strive against this tendency. It has done you harm enough. Make an effort.'

John was irritated.

'I live here on your charity, of course,' he said; 'and the position is enviable. But you can have no more idea of what there is in my heart than of what goes on in the farthest of the stars. You often enough admit that you do not understand me; try to act upon the idea. I drank too much last night. Do you know why? Because I like drinking? Because I was in high spirits, perhaps? Man, you know nothing of sorrow.'

'You may be as sorrowful as you please,' objected Malcolm. 'I am grieved to hear of it. I trust it's through no fault of mine; but surely, surely, that's no reason for—well, for—'

'For making a beast of myself?' suggested John. 'Enough of this,' he added, rising from the table. 'I understand your feeling in this matter. You cannot have a drunkard in the house; of course not. I am not going to promise amendment; I do not aspire so high. But you shall be rid of me to-day.'

'You are speaking in anger, John; in irritation, at least. Do you remember our talk in the avenue on the night of your eighteenth birthday? You said then, what we had often agreed before, that we were to share our fortunes.'

'Green-sickness—romantic boys,' said John, with a wave of his hand.

'You did not think so then, when you had all to expect; nor do I think so now that all is mine. Of course, I have a family; of course, our plans were a little Utopian. But believe me, John, you are doing me the greatest favour in your power by staying here. I respect myself more highly.'

'Oh, if it comes to that—' said John, with a laugh.

'You'll stay?' asked Malcolm, holding out his hand.

'As you will,' replied John, taking it carelessly. 'I own I like my ease; I like gardening and country butter, and the pride of independence I can do without. Besides,' with a sudden change of manner, 'who should have a better right than I?' And with that he went away.

Malcolm shook his head. 'He is not cordial,' he thought. 'There is something between us. I wish I had held my tongue; and yet I can't have him staggering in here at all hours of the morning.'

John went upstairs to a long, low apartment, part lumber-room, part play-room. A considerable library had been brought by Mary Rolland from Hutton at the time of her father's death, but it had never been unpacked until John arrived and offered his services. He went about it leisurely enough; he dallied and lingered over it as a good occupation for wet mornings; and if he ever was two hours on end over his task, for an hour and a-half of that he would be sitting on the floor with some curious book.

An Old Song

The packing-cases were at one end of the room behind a screen; quite at the other end was the fireplace. In about half an hour Mary came in and took a seat by the hearth. John put his head round the end of the screen, wished her a good morning somewhat coldly, and disappeared again. She could hear him take the books out of the case, and lay them on the floor; now and then he cleared his throat. Outside, the rain fell plump and steady; the fire had been lit in honour of the wet day, and the flames prattled pleasantly and the cinders sometimes dropped into the ash-pit. Mary was idly conscious of all these noises: they served her instead of a train of reflection to enliven her work.

John had been silent for some time; he had plainly found something of interest and begun to read, when Mary was startled by a strange sound from behind the screen. It was something between a gasp and a groan. 'What's wrong with him now?' she wondered; but complete silence followed, broken only by the rain and the fire. She became a little uneasy in spite of herself, and again heartily wished that John had never returned to Grangehead.

At last, and rather suddenly, John rose, came round the screen, and advanced towards her with a paper in his hand. But he was no longer the same man; he looked twenty years older—or was it twenty years younger?

'Did you write that?' he asked, hoarsely, as he handed her the paper.

It contained some girlish verses. They were headed, '*To my dear John, on his eighteenth birthday, 12th May, 18—,*' and began, 'Oh, my dear John, I am so fond of you.' It was not the quality of the verse, however, that called the blood up to Mary Falconer's cheek. Her matronly pride was touched; she resented John's emotion like a slur.

'Suppose I did,' she answered, as she threw it straight into the fire; 'what of that?'

'Then you did love me?' he went on.

'You know very well we were engaged,' she answered. 'I hope I have always known my duty' (this with a tremor); 'as long as I was engaged to you, of course I had no thought of anyone else. I cannot conceive what you mean by these questions. It is most unfeeling—most rude.'

John gazed at her with a desolate look in his eyes. 'If I had only known!' he said; 'if I had only, only known!' And then he was silent for awhile. 'But you love your husband now?' he demanded, with sudden fierceness.

'I shall ask you to leave the room, Mr. Falconer,' she said, quivering all over, and making a fine picture of indignation.

'Thank God for that! thank God for that!' he answered, with a sort of laugh. She was unable to move, or she would have quitted the room herself; he looked her all over from head to foot, then he looked into the fire; a little stream of blood began to trickle out of one nostril (he kept the old tendency), but he did not seem to observe the circumstance. At last he turned and went away without a word. At the top of the stairs she heard him slip and fall; he lay for perhaps half a minute; then he picked himself up, went heavily down the steps, and she heard the door close behind him, as he went out.

She recovered herself almost at once. 'Scene or no scene,' she determined, 'he shall not be two days longer in this house.' She had no pity for him; she was conscious of nothing but the offence and the awkwardness. So she determined to be rid of him anyhow; and she was perfectly right. She sought her husband at once.

CHAPTER XII

Poor Malcolm! here was a position, with a vengeance. As he sat, with his uncle's last letter open on his knee, and his wife's words still ringing in his ears, I wonder whether he was not really the most unfortunate of the two. I am sure he thought so himself. What could have tempted John to behave in so absurd a manner? How was he to guess that he had come home drunk on purpose? What was the good of making a kettle of fish like this, instead of letting things go to the devil quietly in their own way? 'Oh!' he cried, finding his old impropriety of expression in the disturbance of the moment, 'confound all your heroes!'

John had a very dismal walk in the rain, and came back from it with the settled intention of leaving Grangehead that evening. The situation could not be prolonged either with dignity or comfort. He asked the servant for Mr. Falconer, and was directed to the library.

Malcolm caught sight of him as he entered, dropped his eyes guiltily upon the table, and made a great show of writing. John walked backwards and forwards behind him, like a caged beast; he, too, had prepared his speech, but there was a ball in his throat. He cleared his throat repeatedly, and at length said—

'John!'

He was rather afraid it had been inaudible, and so he repeated it.

'Eh?' said John, stopping suddenly in his walk.

It was so fiercely spoken, that Malcolm was a little flustered. 'I only wished a word with you,' he answered apologetically. 'Ah!' said John.

Malcolm looked at the paper on which he had been scribbling his own name over and over again to keep up the feint of correspondence. He read all these repetitions from beginning to end, and seemed to feel refreshed. To the last signature he appended his address in a very careful style of penmanship. Then he cleared his throat as if he were going to begin, and fell to examining the nib of the pen upon his thumb-nail.

'Suppose you were to go on,' suggested John.

'Oh, I say, John,' Malcolm dashed into it, with a gasp, I'm very sorry, and—and all that, particularly after what took place this morning; but my wife thinks you had better go away after all—in fact, she insists upon it. Personally, I'm very much disappointed; but of course this kind of thing will happen, I suppose; and—and of course very disagreeable it is. In short—'

He wiped his brow. All his prepared eloquence had deserted him. He was hopelessly entangled, and felt like an imbecile. A curious flame caught his eye and fascinated him at once. He kept staring at it with all his might, telling himself he was thinking what to say next, and not doing so. As he thus sat stupefied, he became conscious, by some electric sympathy, that John was nearer him than he had been, and raised his head with a sudden movement. Their eyes met in the mirror. John's face was deformed with hatred, and in an instant Malcolm's was stricken into the scarcely less hideous image of fear. As they waited, watching each other in the mirror with contracted eyelids, John's hate seemed to increase in proportion with Malcolm's terror, until they looked like a couple of lost spirits.

Malcolm was the first to throw off the spell. With something like a cry he leaped up and turned about as if to defend himself. If he had sat still, nothing in all likelihood would have happened;

but his own action courted an onslaught. Before he had half-faced round, he was forced back against the table; the table upset and, being a light thing, broke in twain between the legs; and the two men fell among its ruins into the hearth. Malcolm was underneath, and his head struck sharply against the iron grate.

When he came to himself, his shirt was loosed, his brow had been wet with ink in default of water, and he was propped upon John's knee.

'Do you feel better?' asked John.

'Why, what's wrong? Why am I here? Where's Mary?'

'Oh, Mary's all right! answered John, bitterly; 'and you're not much worse. You've broken your head, and serve you right! And now, if you please, we'll say good-bye.' He laid Malcolm's head on the floor, and rose to his feet. At the door he turned, and added, in a kinder tone, 'Good-bye, old man.' And with that he was gone.

Malcolm had brown paper and vinegar applied to the back of his head, and was rather sulky all that evening. It rained without intermission, and the roads in that part of the country were hardly passable for travellers on foot.

Edifying Letters
Of The Rutherford Family

LETTER I

William Rutherford to Paul Somerset

Oct. —th 1. A.M.

My dear Paul,

If I only knew where you were, or when you would be anywhere in particular, I could find it in my heart to write you a real, good downright letter in the exhaustive sense and put you in possession of all my last thoughts and adventures. But there is something very chilling in correspondence to a poste restante; to send an arrow to the moon is a hopeless endeavour; but to empty one's spiritual quiver at a moving object is a thing I never will consent to try. The wanderer may plump home upon me the day after I have posted my letter; or he may find it convenient to decamp, drop his address for the moment and make an anonymous dive among the millions of Europe; and there would be all my red hot words left to cool in a dead letter office.

Indeed, letter writing is a terrible venture of a man's soul; and the farther the destination the worse the business is. For you may have changed your mind, or seen reason to feel quite coldly towards your correspondent, long before your production finds its way into his hands. And think how foolish people would look if all their old letters were returned upon them once a year. For my part I think I would rather have my conversation retailed to me; for that comes more freshly; and we scarcely give ourselves time to get completely silly in a talk. But once it comes to pen and ink, and an imperious need for sympathy spurring you up, and a stress of fine language and fine notions, and a late hour of the night with nothing but clocks ticking and stars twinkling all about you—and how you unbutton all your morbid fancies, and give vent to all your silly aspirations and grow young and florid and vehement and gloriously unashamed.

And to think of all this stuff missing its aim, and coming back upon you, like a boomerang, a month afterwards when you are in the cold fit of life! It is like overhearing yourself in the rhapsodies. How very anxious people are to communicate their feelings that they run such risks of mortification! But it is better to do anything than hold your tongue; for I find silence eat into my vitals.

And so, Paul, I care nothing for my part, whether this ever find you, or who reads it. Whoever he is, let me tell him by way of introduction, that I am no fool for my age; and that I write this letter under the pressure of great thoughts. Yes, I'll give that in capitals. Great Thoughts. I do not suppose them to be peculiar to me. I am too old for that. The thoughts that come to persons are of small account; and high ideas fill whole generations and whole races as they struggle towards some adequate expression. I shall never be a great man, although I may have thought so in the past like other boys; I have learned my own measure. I am only a cipher in the sum, a soldier in the vast army of mankind; I am of no account but that I feel the great march music tingling in my blood, and gleefully follow the drums. Is not every woman, for as dull and ugly as she may be in herself, an absorbing piece of nature while she lies in childbed? And so I would say of myself— to you, Paul, if this reach your hands—to you, O fat clerk in the dead letter office, if my cry shall come to no more sympathetic bosom—that I, who am quite a common young man, with no transcendencies to plume myself upon, am something almost sublime for the moment because I am at the height of my position, a young man such as young men ought to be, vehemently scornful of what is past, vehemently aspiring after what is still before.

I am all alone here in the dark; no one is by to encourage or direct me; they all snore and grovel around me on their rubbish heaps, gorged with sawdust and dead verbiage. But I have a light in my heart. I hate falsehood by nature; and I will follow and attain the truth.

Just then a cock crew in the stable lane. I threw open my window, and found the night making ready for the morning; and the whole city dead asleep but the policemen. What a figure of how things are in the spiritual order also! Superstitions outlast their utility like street lamps burning on into the daylight. Nobody is afoot but the Preventive Service—call them the clergy if you like. And still the light grows and grows, and the cocks send up their signals, only listened to by wakeful youth.

Looking back on what I have written, I came upon a word that staggered me. I said I hated falsehood by nature. Indeed, and so I do. I will have the heart out of the truth; I will not go on any longer in this vain show; I feel as if the wisdom I have been taught is no more than shadows and a jargon; and I will be out of it all and see things face to face, or no longer carry about with me this dishonourable life. And yet, my dear Paul, I am a liar. This is an ugly quandary for a man to be in. I profess such high notions, do I? and meanwhile my practice is all in the mud. A liar, that is what I am—an habitual and conscious liar.

Why, no later ago than this evening, I was at it; and that on such a small occasion as makes me truly ashamed to confess. For it was about nothing more serious than our old chronic irritation of late hours. I do not think we are ever likely to get done with this quarrel, at least as long as the clocks go so fast whenever I am out of the house, or so long as I am so anxious to avoid them and they keep so resolute to sit up for me. For really I fancy they must do it on purpose. I may come in when I please, they are up and broad awake; I apply my stealthy pass key in the small hours and behold the dining room is lighted up like day, and there is a domestic group about the fireplace, waiting in rosy respectability for the prodigal. This is a sort of anti-climax that my soul cannot abide. I may have been out all night climbing the heavens of invention, drinking deep, thinking high; I go home, with my heart stirred to all its depths and my brain sparkling like wine and starlight; I open a door, and the whole of this gaudy and light-hearted life must pass away in a moment, and give place to a few words of course and a pair of formal kisses. The sky-raker must give some account of his evening, if you please; and the spirit which has just been reconstructing the universe and debating the attributes of God, must bring down its proud stomach, and screw up its somewhat hazy eyes, to read a chapter from the authorised version of the Holy Bible! To be thus knocked off the apex of apotheosis, and sent to bed with a renewed sense of all one's troubles and sober after all, is, as Butler would say, a sheer waste of drink.

Butler, by the bye, is the very man I was with this evening. I met him at the station, where we had a true starry night of intellect and sherry. We pulled about the infinites at a great rate, I can promise you; and undermined Society from end to end, until it seemed as if we had only to lift up our voices for the whole pasteboard Jericho to crash together and tumble in the dust. We kept going out and in between the platform and the bar, the one with its cool and solemn spaces, and here and there a bit of a bustle and a night train preparing to flame forth on its adventurous journey—the other with all its lights and coloured bottles and redheaded barmaids. Both Butler and I delight greatly in these contrasts, which keep a man conscious of either pole of his being; like a town and a country life; or love and sea bathing; or Shakespeare and Voltaire. And we pleased ourselves besides with elaborate pieces of childishness; making believe that we were going to start with all the trains, and looking forward to the pleasant waking in a new place with new air to breathe and a new accent in people's speech; making believe, by the slender aid of a marble table, that this refreshment bar was a Parisian Café, and we were free people with our pockets full of gold; making believe, in short, in all sorts of ways, that we had slipped the leash, and were gotten clean away out of our old life and out into the world as young men ought to be, among their rivals and their aspirations. In Paris we ordered many choice little dinners, went to many different plays at different theatres and laid out some very gay evenings in imagination; and I declare the whole thing so grew upon my mind that I went home quite flushed with the idea that I was indeed free, and could come and go at my own will. I need not tell you which would be my first movement, Paul Somerset; for go I emphatically should; I am like a bird in a cage, like a prisoner in his cell; just let me see a crevice, and I will show my heels to this dismal city in a trice, and land where the sun shines and neighbours mind their own business. Perhaps there is no such place, no such place, all the wide world over; and nothing but rain and carping and sour looks, and the damned wearisome ten commandments, and their ten million corollaries, dinned in people's ears to perpetuity. There's always the grave, Paul; the grave where the sabbath bells are silent; the grave, where the elders cease from troubling and the wicked are at rest.

As I was saying, I went home in a fine tip-toe transcendental frame of mind, all golden credulity, golden outlooks on the future, and the blue sky of liberty overhead. And when I had deftly turned the passkey, and thought to slip off to bed and trail all these clouds of glory direct into my dreams, what should I find but the house all lit up from top to bottom, and the sound of knives and forks in the dining room. I hate late hours on the part of my superiors!—Gregory it seems had dropped in on some business, and they had given him a late supper.

87

I buttoned myself together as best I could and took a place at table. My father looked a little lowering, my mother a bit anxious; the uncalled for Gregory smiled and ate, unconscious of the threatening weather.

'You are late,' said my father. 'Where have you been?'

I gave the first excuse that came into my head, and told him I had been at the Theatre to hear the Grande Duchesse. I declare when they ask me these pistolling questions, I would rather tell them anything but the truth; I will not tell the truth upon compulsion; and I hate to tell the truth about my own life anyway, unless it come spontaneously, and I am on the openest terms with the person to whom I tell it; the least suspicion of strain or misconstruction, the least shade of authority, and my mouth is closed. But on this occasion I had to pay for my refinements pretty dear. For no sooner had I said I had been at the theatre, than out came Gregory with a smile.

'Were you?' says he. 'Why, so was I!'

'Mr. Gregory has been here this half hour,' said my mother. 'How come you to be so much behind him?'

'I suppose he didn't sit it out,' returned I.

'Ah, but I did though,' cries Gregory—'to the bitter end.'

My father looked at me more heavily than ever, and his resemblance to my grandfather's bust became appalling. I murmured something about seeing a fellow home. I think my mother must have been struck with the discrepancy of my two answers; and with the natural leniency of women towards falsehood, cut in at once to protect me from further badgering in that direction. For she demanded in quite an animated manner, who it was that I had seen home. She really could not have cared greatly for an answer; but it cost me dear to give her one. I first thought of naming Butler, from the wish of a person in my circumstances to get some little patch of truth into his inventions; but I remembered how often he meets my father in the morning and fearing

88

some clashing of evidence, in a bold spirit, I created a personage for my use.

'A fellow McDowel,' said I, 'a medical student.' And I was conscious of blushing as I said it.

I hoped I was through the wood then; but my fate was not yet weary; the accursed Gregory had yet another arrow in his quiver. He asked me in what part of the house I had been; and when I risked the stalls, 'So was I!' cried he. 'How odd I didn't see you!'

And then you can imagine how I bogged myself in all sorts of difficulties about the righthand of the actors and the right hand of the audience, about the number of benches counted from the front and the number of benches counted from the back; and with what sort of hang dog looks I finally issued from the discussion. They must, I say they must have observed my tribulation. My face was the colour of beet-root and my shirt was all damp in the inside; and I had to feign sleep and slink off to my own room, to put a period to my confusion. Will they remark upon it in the morning, I wonder? I wish I was dead, Paul Somerset. A man of my high-looking aspirations caught wriggling in such pitiful imbroglios! A person who speaks such big words across the dinner-table, taken in petty falsehood over supper! Think of it, for God's sake, and tell me what it means.

After such humiliations, I feel inclined to give it all up and drink myself comfortably to death like my betters. What is the good of making an elaborate toilette when one has a humpback? Humpbacked you must remain. Yes, but the humpback may have a true heart about him: the liar may go to the stake; the coward may renew the hearts of heroes with brave words. There is nothing quite useless in the world except stupidity; and even that may dance profitably enough upon the treadmill. I who am daily making allowances for others, may surely treat myself to a little of my own toleration and take the benefit of my own theories, may I not? or there's no justice in life, and no good theorising.

Good bye, Paul. Write soon, and I'll answer. I am full of matter like a champagne bottle; and like all persons lying in a state of siege, I have plenty of incidents from day to day to chronicle. Do you wish the history? The Siege of Mansoul, by a beleaguered Resident, with an appendix on the intestine broils and revolutions. The world is all a war to me, where I lose battles and lose honour daily. I am sick and I wish you were home.

ever yours,
W. Rutherford

LETTER II

*Mr. Rutherford to Professor Daubeny Fisher
in the University of Aberdeen*

My dear Daubeny,

I am sure you will be very sorry to hear of poor Nathaniel's illness. There is now little hope of his recovery according to the doctors; and I wish I could report better of his spiritual health, which seems to be in as doubtful a state as the other. He has spat a great deal of blood lately, poor fellow. When I went to see him the other day, he seemed quite conscious that he was nearing the end, but I could get no satisfaction when I spoke to him. To look about his rooms, with his foils hanging up, and his prints (more or less indecent according to me) upon the walls and his tobacco pipes over the chimney, really cut me to the heart. The notions of death and of a man's last smoke have got inextricably connected in my mind; and when I thought that poor Nathaniel had very likely taken his last whiff, I found it almost a harder task than I was able for, to speak to him of indifferent subjects and try to keep his spirits up. Of serious matters, he would hear nothing; at least, he would hear nothing from me; but that, of course, does not mean so much; for you know my miserable weakness on such occasions, and how much I hate even the least shadow of cant.

And yet surely in the presence of the King of Terrors, such nonsensical feelings (for nonsensical they are) ought to be laid aside. The time will come for all of us to *get into bed for the last time;* and I feel sure we shall be most obliged at such a time to those of our friends who are most plain-spoken. Life will cut a very poor figure; and Eternity look perhaps as ugly as it must always be momentous.

After I had seen Nathaniel I walked round the Calton Hill with the dogs, in a very dispirited temper. Of course, I was reminded at every turn of our old doings as high school boys; but as often as I was inclined to smile, the thought of that *poor fellow who has smoked his last pipe,* came into my head and spoiled the joke. We are neither of us young men, my dear Daubeny; the body is beginning to wear threadbare; and soon the hearse will be at the door, plumes and all! We have all had our Saturday Holidays; but to think of that poor Nathaniel and *his* Saturday holidays really comes between me and my work. I could not help moralising rather bitterly over the body, which is such a bad companion through so much of life, and makes such an uncomfortable bedfellow as death approaches. I pray God with all my heart for all people who are beginning to go down; it is a sad trial, without Christ's grace. Think, Daubeny, of *seeing the gas lit for the last time,* some gurly, gousty winter afternoon. I have heard people boasting of courage for such circumstances, but I doubt if anybody's blood would not run cold, even of the most faithful Christians.

William has several classes at the University this session; but I am more than doubtful whether he gives his mind to the business in hand. I am afraid he has an *ex*cursive and *dis*cursive mind, tending to nothing in particular. I see no signs of steady work, although much desultory reading. You are brought so much into contact with young men by your university position, that I often envy your experience and sometimes feel inclined to consult it. It is a terrible responsibility before God and one's own heart, to have the upbringing of an only child; and Nathaniel's illness, which I am afraid has cast a gloom over all my letter, has made me consider this more seriously than I think I have ever done before. I thought of my brother, and I was indeed harassed by the thought. How would that *truly Christian man* have been cast down, to see his son go towards death with a thoroughly pagan carelessness and (if I may say so) equally without hope or fear? A father must surely rank very low and feel with great bitterness, if he finds himself in the Kingdom of Heaven and all his offspring *elsewhere*. But I have great hopes of William. He keeps irregular hours, but we have all been young, and we know that many things come right by the mere course of time. And I believe he is the son of my own heart in many particulars; above all in one; that he would never tell me what was false. When he was quite a child, I had several alarms about him on this head; but he has quite outgrown the fault; and I can rely entirely on his lightest expression. Moreover, as I have always laid myself out to be his *friend* rather than his *father* (perhaps wrongly), I feel sure there is no unnatural *strain* in our relations, and that he can speak to me with perfect ease and freedom. Still, the turn of youth is a ticklish time. So perhaps is the turn of *age*, Daubeny; and perhaps we all require to give and take a little.

My new dog sends his most respectful compliments to your new one. Mine is called Fin McCoul: he seems stupid, but amiable and honest. Youth, and Saturday Holidays, and a dog worth his shot, are things that come no more. I suppose we must all become *laudatores temporis acti* and *canum actarum*, which is, I fancy, and quite properly too, *dog* latin. But I am happy to remember that I have been a conservative all my days, which makes the situation less humiliating for me than it might be for many others. With affectionate regards, believe me, yours most affectionately

James Rutherford

Prof. D. Fisher.
&c. &c. &c.

LETTER III

William Rutherford to Charles Butler

My dear Charles,

God help me, if I know what to do with myself this morning. I am high and dry. The waters have gone down on all sides and left me stranded on my beam ends upon an illimitable quicksand. I am as fond of humanity as I was last night, and I have aims of the highest practicable or impracticable order; but my brain, my dear Charles, is a torrid desert—but my head, my dear Charles, is a belfry, where innumerable insane bellringers leap and swing and bob up and down upon excruciating bellropes. I stopped and listened to the air just now; I suppose it must be what they call a triple bob major. When they strike on a fine, deep, sonorous boom, like a crooning stock dove, I can dominate the agony and contain my spirit; but when they fly off into a treble clang with a shrill chord in it, it seems to me as if my sutures were uncemented, and my ribs unjointed, and my little, bare, blind, naked, immortal spirit went floating up and away into death-in-life and the inter-stellar spaces. All the time, the feet of the demon bellringers go flitting and skipping to and fro on the unhappy belfry floor; and every step is agony to me.

In short, I have neuralgia.

Only, it happens to be better just now and leaves me a lucid interval for conversation with a friend some streets away. God bless the penny postman. You will either answer or call, will you not?

This notion of mine about my head being a trampled and reverberating belfry, full of leaping bellringers and clangorous bells, has got between me and my healthy wits, I think. First, it led me on to the idea of such an expanse of green and quiet country as may be seen from many an English bell-tower; and so to the belief that all the world was silent and fresh and sweet, except that little temple of discord and agony, my tormented skull. And second, I got thinking, how my life was noisy and rude like the belfry and other people's lives pleasant like the country round about. And third, I remembered how the bells, which sounded so harshly near at hand, sang as sweet as birds in the distance. And so from that, I came on to the grand conviction that out of this neuralgic head, there would go forth something helpful and supporting to mankind, for ever and ever, world without end, amen.

I don't know what 'world without end, amen' means; but then no more do you. And besides I was drunk last night, and so do not require to be logical.

The world is quite mad, Butler, all except you and me. Paul Somerset, also, you will find to have some little golden grains of sanity in his soul, so soon as he returns from the Pyrenees and I shall be able to present you to each other. As for the poor creatures whom we have persuaded—bribed, shall I say?—to join in our society, for the sake of the beer and the liberty of language, they are not fit companions for us. But even the swift beating heart of the eagle must carry its tucked feet behind it into the heavens. If an army could consist of the generals alone, there would be battles fought to put history to the blush.

[For the title:—Liberty seems right—is the true blue, at least; youth's watchword, the gist of hope. Justice—which means the liberty of others—is quite as good. But where the devil, Butler, got ye Reverence? I will admit that 'L. J. R.' is a pleasant monogram to put upon our tankards. But what, in the name of Beelzebub, have we to do with Reverence? What is Reverence?]

I am going to set to work upon the constitution tonight, if my head allows me. There seems to me to be some fine sentences in what you have drafted; but a little want of solid, constructive ideas; indeed there are so few of these that I had a humourous idea that it was hardly worth while founding a society on such a little bit of cobweb. Liberty, Justice, and so forth—why, damn it, Butler, these are everybody's watchwords. The elder, the clergyman, the hereditary noble, all the swine and wolves of Europe cry Liberty and Justice in their moments. There would be a good opening for something a trifle more specific in our program; but that will come, I daresay, in time and by talking. We admitted, the other afternoon, that the first business we should have to attend to, was to educate our fellow members. Perhaps we shall really have to begin a step farther back, by educating ourselves. In the meantime, we have generous aspirations and ample faith; and that seems to me a pretty good stock in trade for a political society. [Nay, and I am most ungrateful; we have our tankard also, with the monogram carefully engraved; and we have our hall of convocation in a part of the town so low as to merit the name (to coin a singular) of a 'purlieu.' Someday, we shall have black masques and skulls and corresponding members, and a real mission.] People don't wait until they are thrown off of shipboard, to purchase life-preservers or learn to swim; and so we also; let us have the disciples ready and the church organised; and sooner or later, who knows, but the gospel may make its appearance.

[I gave a look again over our notes, and I see I have been shamefully unjust. There is stuff in them; there are principles laid down there, Charles Butler, which, I am not ashamed to say, since after all they spring originally from neither you nor me, if they were once embraced, would turn this world into a garden. The essentials of liberty, the . . .]

Talking of the gospel, puts me in mind of something I had meant to tell you at full length when we met, but which I suppose I may as well set on paper at once. My only literary aspiration is to leave as much as possible of my life in my friends' letter boxes; some of these days, when I have had a severe illness and come to myself in the beautiful early springtime, I shall collect my correspondence from the four winds, and prop myself up with pillows to live my hot youth over again in fancy. Picture it, O Butler,—O thou, who manufacturest reminiscences!—is that not an idea after thine own heart? I mean to begin in the morning, with the dew not yet shaken from the lilac flowers; sounds of country life shall come to me in the clear hush; the birds are to be all in admirable voice and all of one opinion about the unsurpassable weather; a little flutter of wind is to run in from time to time at the open window and just stir the letters on my lap; and when I turn my head a little, I am to see a bit of folded valley, with a church spire upon the sky. I will go a little farther, if you like; for luxuries cost nothing in a fancy piece. I will have a corner of fallow land within view, on a hillside; and there shall go a-ploughing, a big, cheery-throated fellow with a pair of lusty horses and a vortex of crows behind him. And now, with these surroundings, and in that frame of crystalline transparency of mind and body that follows upon a great sickness, to have all one's old sorrows and joys, winter afternoons, roaring nights, spring vigils, all the grimy and beautiful stuff that goes to build up the dream that men call their youth, pass before you bit by bit in your own language of the moment— to have your old thoughts 'take a new acquaintance of your mind' as Shakespeare advises (and surely he was a good adviser)—to look back up the road of life and see yourself, as in one of these jolly old pictorial maps of the Pilgrim's Progress, now here, now there, a little figure dwindling and dwindling down into the past—I am sure for my part that it would be twice the pleasure and not one half the pain of the actual rude living it. People say it is unlike youth to care about the past; we two must be very old then; you, who would always prefer a reminiscence to a glass of wine; I, who have been writing all this nonsense—not to you, do not flatter yourself—you are no more than a repository or sort of postal system—but to my own self twenty years hereafter, propped up on pillows by the open window.

Well, to go on, my poor father took it into his head that I should go with him and see my cousin Nathaniel. The goodman is, as you know, a great believer in deathbed scenery; and Nath is in the Dark Valley with a vengeance for himself and many circumstances of aggravation for the spectator. He seems to have most known maladies, poor devil; and his cough has nearly killed *me* in a single morning call, so that I can judge what it must be for him all night and all day long. I have a great dislike to see slight empty characters placed in these grave situations. I think I have told you before what a shock I had, when that butterfly Mrs. A died in childbed. Well, Nath is a stronger case; he is really of such small account as a fellow creature, that he seems unfit for dying altogether; the part is too serious for him; he is in his place well enough in a tea party, but to think of him alone in the Dark Valley! I feel choked with a sort of sobbing laughter at the thought. I could find it in my heart to jeer at him and cry over him in the same breath. Persons, whom you have always unwaveringly despised and hated, seem to put you in a false position when they come to die.

The poor fellow was propped up in bed when we went in, and looked very lamentable against the green bed curtains. I noticed by my father's manner and the knowledge he seemed to have, that he must call nearly every day; which is indeed good of him, and like him; for you remember how he used to look down upon Nath in his better days. He professed himself overjoyed to see me, which I am afraid was a lie; and he must have found it difficult to articulate, for it set him coughing for quite a while, my father and I standing awkwardly before him until he was done. If it had not been for the pity of the thing, I believe we should have broken out laughing at each other, we both looked so foolish.

'You don't know how tired of himself, a fellow gets lying here,' he said. 'I declare if ever I get well, which is damned unlikely, I shall take to visiting the sick.' This probably is the only speech of Nath's in all his life that can be recorded to his credit; my father had not the heart to reprove him for the oath, although I could see he would have dearly liked. I could find nothing to say; I felt so ashamed of myself for hating him when he was sick, for one thing; and for another, when a fellow is quite deadly stupid, and absolutely corrupt in every thought, and has not a week to live, I should like to know what is the appropriate vein to talk to him in. I suppose perhaps it is the one my father chose; for down he sat by him; and prattled a sort of grown-up baby-talk, about dogs, and the weather and the man in the moon: a great deal about the man in the moon, for instance, and humourous enough it was. I can't think how he kept it up; for I could see his heart was just broken all the time; and I could have fallen on his neck and wept. This sort of pitiful cheerfulness is of all things the most moving to me; and what with that and the cough-coughing of the invalid, I really felt as if I was going out of my wits. My embarrassment ran so high that I took refuge in the first book that came under my hand. It happened to be the New Testament; and I own that cast me down a little at first. People who have had the Bible so assiduously rung in upon them from the cradle upwards as you and I, will jib a little at any symptom of a new infliction. But just at the first pitch, I set my eyes on a passage that seemed to stand out of the paper. It was about God sending the sun and rain upon the just and the unjust indifferently and it gave me some new thoughts about Christ and what is called Christianity, which I mean to investigate at leisure. All great men are perhaps after the same end, about the same multisided business; and Christ and us, Wordsworth and Byron, Venus and Diana, may be all of a side, if we could only see the contrary; for you know how split up a party seems, until we can compare it with the other. Perhaps this is going to be the Gospel. Talk of faith, I am the true faithful. It is not possible that any man should be so anxious to do right as I am and not find a sufficient guide.

When the visit was over, my father and I got out into the street, and I hastened to excuse myself and slip away. My conscience smote me a little; for I saw he had set his heart on walking with me. But how could I dare? I tell you frankly, Charles, if I had not felt as kindly towards him, if he had not touched me so nearly by his gentleness with Nath, I might have risked a walk with him; but as things are, I could trust neither him nor myself; we should have been safe to grow confidential; and confidence, where there is so great a gulf in sympathy, means quarrelling. So I had to let him go on alone with the dogs, while I took refuge in a tobacconist's shop. Of course, with the admirable instinct of a father, he will misunderstand me and be bitterly offended. But that is what life is. Now I wonder how people manage with their wives; if they're anything like parents, give me white feathers and the tomb.

Write or call, like a good soul.

Yours ever
Willm Rutherford

LETTER IV

William Rutherford to Paul Somerset

I had a strange waking vision this morning, my dear Paul, which has put me in a very high frame of mind. You know how the idea of dawn runs in my head. Well, it seemed to me that I rose pretty early, went over many little dewy meadows and by watercourses and willowwoods, and at length scaled a little hill and began to look about me in the gray of the morning. The height on which I stood was in itself inconsiderable, but by reason of its position in the bottom of a vast amphitheatre of highlands, it gave me a spacious outlook all around. The mists were lifting out of the hollows; the cocks were crowing in the steading yards; a tremor ran among the hills. And suddenly, the sun took hold upon one mountain top, and then of another, and began to spread out from peak to peak, and gush over through the breaches; until the whole amphitheatre brimmed with broad daylight and shadows.

That was the figure, and the rough substance; but how I am to tell you what I thought I saw along with all this, I do not know. For wherever this daylight fell, a joy seemed to come out of the earth; peace and glory possessed the world; injustice and tyranny and feverish thoughts seemed to pass away in the twinkling of an eye and forever, like swift birds. It was Kingdom Come; it was El Dorado, Astraea Redux: what you please. But my heart leaped up, and my clay seemed purged and quickened and sat more lightly on my thoughts.

Perhaps I am not a prophet; but then perhaps I am: the spirit of prophecy has no diagnostic symptoms like the measles. And at least, since I fancied I saw into the future, let me write the fancies down.

I saw people sitting, each in his garden, or roaming alone on woody hilltops whence they might perceive the sea; and each was poor, and happy and content. Not a man but was in rags; and the women too were clad poorly. When the dinner was cooked they ran out pressing their neighbours to come in; and the limping passer by, who was on some long journey and browned with noon in many another land, entered like an invited guest and took his place among the children. One man, methought, had a library of books, and I saw him hurry to and fro in the village, pressing others to borrow. Another, for some great service to the state, had been rewarded with a fortune unusual in that age; he seemed happy like a child; his eyes smiled like an angel's; with a great purse, he kept running from door to door, and wherever there was a want to satisfy, he offered many smiling . . .

(Stevenson's manuscript ends here, and was never finished.)